A Gospel Worthy Of Your Life

Orienting every resource, attitude and passion around the Cross

Bill Mills

Foreword by Craig Parro
Study Guide by Rachel Atkison

A Gospel Worthy of Your Life: Orienting Every Resource, Attitude and Passion Around the Cross by Bill Mills

Foreword by Craig Parro
Study Guide by Rachel Atkison

Copyright © Leadership Resources 2018
12575 Ridgeland Avenue, Palos Heights, IL 60463

Print ISBN: 978-1939707352
EBook ISBN: 978-1939707369

This ministry is dedicated to:

The Glory of God
The Honor of His Word
The Building Up of the Body of Christ

Only let your manner of life be worthy of the gospel of Christ, so that whether I come and see you or am absent, I may hear of you that you are standing firm in one spirit, with one mind striving side by side for the faith of the gospel,

Philippians 1:27

Table of Contents

Craig Parro

President of Leadership Resources

Y ou are about to enter the realm of "simple, but profound." Surely you've already discovered that many of life's greatest treasures are simple, but profound. The gospel, for one. The way we live our lives in response to the gospel, for another.

Too often we overcomplicate the good news of the gospel and the Christian life that flows out of that gospel. Bill Mills' latest book provides a helpful corrective as he unpacks Paul's epistle to the Philippians. Bill makes clear that the message of Philippians is both simple and profound.

How are two women who are fighting among themselves supposed to resolve their irreconcilable differences? "Agree with one another." Really??? It's that simple??? How are we to get over our personal guilt, disappointments and failures? "Forget what lies behind." "But, wait a minute," we protest, "you don't understand..." This study of Philippians prompts a troubling question: does our desire to nuance our problems simply mask our unbelief?

In this book you'll discover simple but profound answers to life's challenges, but you won't find "the balanced Christian life." Bill lays bare the fallacy of this noble-sounding idea that proves to have no biblical warrant. "Moderation" is exposed as a convenient cop-out. A life worthy of the gospel doesn't carefully measure out; instead it pours out until there's nothing left, and in the process, discovers life that is life indeed!

Though Bill Mills has written over a dozen books, this book is his best, the distillation of over 50 years of faithful ministry. If you've read Bill's other books, you'll hear echoes of past themes. But you'll also discover precious new insights into the heart of God, not the least of which is his preference for mercy over justice.

Be prepared to have a number of your assumptions about God and living God's way challenged. Also, be prepared to grow more fully into the image of Christ and experience more fully the joy of the Lord. Finally, as you complete this book, be prepared to worship our great God and Savior who gave Himself for us in order to reconcile us to Himself. Worthy is the Lamb that was slain!

Craig Parro
President of Leadership Resources

Introduction

In his letter to the Church at Philippi, the Apostle Paul calls his beloved brothers and sisters to "Let their manner of life be worthy of the gospel of Christ" (Philippians 1:27). One of God's great gifts to them, and to us as we follow this same call, is that He has given us a gospel worthy of our lives! The wonderful good news of God's grace to us in Christ Jesus is worthy of all that we are and all that we have—every resource, every relationship, every attitude of our heart, and every passion of our soul.

Thank you for joining me as we walk through this beautiful letter that Paul wrote to the church that he loved more deeply than any other in all of his missionary journeys. They supported him financially, they prayed for him, and perhaps even most importantly, they joined with him in his sufferings and his defense of the gospel. Paul's affections were bound up in his brothers and sisters in Philippi who shared his love for the Lord Jesus.

As he began this letter, Paul made clear his desire that they would experience the very things that come only from the heart of our God, His grace and His peace:

Grace to you and peace from God our Father and the Lord Jesus Christ. (Philippians 1:2)

NEW BIRTHS IN GOD'S SOVEREIGN GRACE

We find the beginnings of this amazing church in the book of Acts. Paul and Barnabas had completed their first missionary journey with the incredible response of the Gentiles to the hope of repentance and faith in Christ. The council of elders and apostles at Jerusalem had affirmed together in the Holy Spirit that salvation comes not through keeping the works of the Law, but through God's grace alone: God's Word was moving through Asia!

> But we believe that we will be saved through the grace of the Lord Jesus, just as they will. (Acts 15:11)

Now, Paul desired to return with Barnabas to the churches God had raised up through their preaching and shepherding. He wanted to see how they were doing, and to encourage them to remain strong in the faith:

> And after some days Paul said to Barnabas, "Let us return and visit the brothers in every city where we proclaimed the word of the Lord, and see how they are." (Acts 15:36)

There was a dispute between Paul and Barnabas about whether to take John Mark with them once again. Paul felt that since Mark had left them and the work while they were in Pamphylia, it would not be wise to bring him with them on this next trip. Barnabas felt strongly that he should join with them once again. The dispute was so strong that Paul decided to take Silas with him, and Barnabas took Mark with him to Cyprus. While Paul and Silas were in Derbe and Lystra, they were joined by a young disciple of Paul named Timothy.

As Paul, Timothy, Silas and Luke (the author of Acts) were going through Galatia (modern Turkey), Paul had a vision of a man from Macedonia (modern Greece):

> And a vision appeared to Paul in the night: a man of Macedonia was standing there, urging him and saying, "Come over to Macedonia and help us." And when Paul had seen the vision, immediately we sought to go on into

Macedonia, concluding that God had called us to preach the gospel to them. (Acts 16:9–10)

God brought the brothers to the city of Philippi, which was a leading city in Macedonia and a Roman colony. Not too long after their arrival, the missionary team was seeking a quiet place to pray, and there they met Lydia, a gracious and successful businesswoman. Luke describes her conversion in this way:

> And after she was baptized, and her household as well, she urged us, saying, "If you have judged me to be faithful to the Lord, come to my house and stay." And she prevailed upon us. As we were going to the place of prayer, we were met by a slave girl who had a spirit of divination and brought her owners much gain by fortune-telling. (Acts 16:15–16)

As Paul and the team continued to preach Christ, a riot broke out over a slave girl who was possessed with a spirit of divination. She kept crying out that these men were preaching the truth, but she became such a distraction to Paul that he cast the spirit out of her. Her owners, however, now facing the loss of the money they were making from their use of her, started a riot. Paul and his brothers ended up in the city jail! What did they do next?

> About midnight Paul and Silas were praying and singing hymns to God, and the prisoners were listening to them. (Acts 16:25)

God loosened the chains of all the prisoners through a great earthquake, and the jailer was about to kill himself. Paul, however, assured him that all of the prisoners were still there, and pleaded with him not to harm himself.

> Then he brought them out and said, "Sirs, what must I do to be saved?" And they said, "Believe in the Lord Jesus, and you will be saved, you and your household." And they spoke the word of the Lord to him and to all who were in his house. (Acts 16:30–32)

11

In response to the hope of life and salvation in the Son of God, the jailer and his entire household believed. They were baptized, and the church in Philippi was born! The new birth of Lydia, the jailer and his family, and the church that God would use so greatly in the gospel and in Paul's life and ministry—all are the result of God's sovereign grace and mercy.

> And he took them the same hour of the night and washed their wounds; and he was baptized at once, he and all his family. Then he brought them up into his house and set food before them. And he rejoiced along with his entire household that he had believed in God. But when it was day, the magistrates sent the police, saying, "Let those men go." (Acts 16:33–35)

PROCLAIMING THE GOSPEL IN WORD AND ACTION

So it is with you and me. The God who had appointed the times, places and circumstances of the Philippian jailer in order to bring him and his family to Himself has done that with us. Just as God opened Lydia's heart to respond to the gospel, His grace also drew us to His Son. And just as God called Paul, Barnabas, Silas, Timothy and Luke to spread the gospel of Jesus to the entire known world, He has committed the message of reconciliation to you and me.

> Therefore, we are ambassadors for Christ, God making his appeal through us. We implore you on behalf of Christ, be reconciled to God. For our sake he made him to be sin who knew no sin, so that in him we might become the righteousness of God. (2 Corinthians 5:20–21)

That is the gospel! God took our sin and placed it on Christ, and then took His righteousness and placed it on us, so that we might be in a right relationship with Him, become His children and live with Him forever. We carry this message of hope wherever we go, to all who will listen, knowing that God is at work reconciling a broken and dying world to Himself through the death of His Son.

> For God so loved the world, that he gave his only Son, that whoever believes in him should not perish but have eternal life. (John 3:16)

As we walk through Philippians, we will talk much about how we carry this gospel to the world. We will obviously talk about communicating the hope of salvation through God's work of redemption in the cross and our faith in Him. That our sins can be forgiven, that we can live in relationship with our heavenly Father now through the Holy Spirit and in Him share the confidence of eternal life, is the hope this world needs to hear.

It is clear when we look at the ministry of the Lord Jesus that the gospel is carried not only by words, but also by attitudes and actions. Our attitudes that reveal the heart of Jesus, our relationships that reflect the transformation we preach, our heart for the poor, and our commitment to justice and mercy for the oppressed, all are part of proclaiming the gospel. It is a great testimony to God's message of grace in Christ that the great social awakenings of England and America, whether care for the poor and oppressed, ending the horror of slavery or confronting the heinous sin of racism, have been led by those who bear the name of Jesus.

Our call in the gospel is more than inviting people we meet to receive Jesus Christ as Lord and Savior. Our ministry is to proclaim the entire message of the New Covenant, which fulfills the Old Covenant that revealed the holiness and the heart of our God. The gospel is seen in the Old Testament as it so clearly points to Christ, and also as it shows how God's priorities are seen in the lives of His people. In addition to believing in Him, walking in obedience, and placing their hope for deliverance in His great power, God made clear His commitment to the poor and oppressed.

> Is not this the fast that I choose: to loose the bonds of wickedness, to undo the straps of the yoke, to let the oppressed go free, and to break every yoke? Is it not to share your bread with the hungry and bring the homeless poor into your house; when you see the naked, to cover him, and not to hide yourself from your own flesh? (Isaiah 58:6–7)

In Jesus's earthly ministry, He fully revealed His Father's glory and character to us. A major aspect of that revelation was seen in His heart for the poor and oppressed, the sick and the sinful. As we proclaim who Jesus is and the gospel that bears His name, God's heart for hurting people will be a major aspect of our proclamation. We can see vividly in Jesus's ministry how He fulfilled His Father's priorities of justice and mercy:

> "With what shall I come before the LORD, and bow myself before God on high? Shall I come before him with burnt offerings, with calves a year old? Will the LORD be pleased with thousands of rams, with ten thousands of rivers of oil? Shall I give my firstborn for my transgression, the fruit of my body for the sin of my soul?" He has told you, O man, what is good; and what does the LORD require of you but to do justice, and to love kindness, and to walk humbly with your God? (Micah 6:6–8)

CARRYING THE GOSPEL IN THE
POWER OF THE NEW COVENANT

A major part of Paul's second letter to the church at Corinth was his teaching on the hope and the power of the New Covenant for us as believers. This teaching came in the context of defending himself as an apostle. Some of the leaders in Corinth put him in that position by comparing him with the "super apostles" (2 Corinthians 12:11–13).

> Are we beginning to commend ourselves again? Or do we need, as some do, letters of recommendation to you, or from you? You yourselves are our letter of recommendation, written on our hearts, to be known and read by all. And you show that you are a letter from Christ delivered by us, written not with ink but with the Spirit of the living God, not on tablets of stone but on tablets of human hearts. (2 Corinthians 3:1–3)

The focus of Paul's defense is the work that God had done in their hearts through his ministry. He describes that eternal work as a "letter written in their hearts." As Paul talks of letters written in hearts by the Spirit and those written on tablets of stone, he is contrasting two covenants: the covenant of the Law, and the New Covenant of life in Christ through the Holy Spirit!

> Such is the confidence that we have through Christ toward God. Not that we are sufficient in ourselves to claim anything as coming from us, but our sufficiency is from God, who has made us sufficient to be ministers of a new covenant, not of the letter but of the Spirit. For the letter kills, but the Spirit gives life. (2 Corinthians 3:4–6)

One of the most wonderful changes for you and me as we enter into this New Covenant relationship with God through faith in His Son is that our resources for all that God gives us to do, and all of life, no longer come from ourselves, but from Him. We live every day, and face every situation, with the power of the risen Christ! We walk every moment in the Spirit who gives life, rather than in the law that brings death.

> Now if the ministry of death, carved in letters on stone, came with such glory that the Israelites could not gaze at Moses' face because of its glory, which was being brought to an end, will not the ministry of the Spirit have even more glory? (2 Corinthians 3:7–8)

Is it not interesting that Paul does not continue to focus on his own defense as an apostle, but is rather caught up in the hope, power and glory of Christ and the New Covenant? The glory of the law faded away, but the gospel has glory that remains. That glory flows from the message the New Covenant proclaims:

> For if there was glory in the ministry of condemnation, the ministry of righteousness must far exceed it in glory. Indeed, in this case, what once had glory has come to have no glory at all, because of the glory that surpasses it. (2 Corinthians 3:9–10)

The Old Covenant was a "ministry of condemnation," Paul says. Now, through the death and resurrection of Christ, who bore our sins and His Father's condemnation toward us at the cross, God gives us His own Son's righteousness when we believe what He has done and place our faith in Him.

> For if what was being brought to an end came with glory, much more will what is permanent have glory. (2 Corinthians 3:11)

The glory of the New Covenant is the hope of the believer, and it is the fuel that moves those who carry its message! Paul is seeking to capture the hearts of his readers in Philippi for the gospel, and his appeal is through this very glory revealed in the beauty and surpassing worthiness of God's own Son, Jesus. May the beauty and glory of Christ fuel the passions of our souls as well, as we live lives worthy of His gospel, and carry the good news of the cross to our families, our neighbors, and the ends of the earth.

WHY I WROTE THIS BOOK

As I studied Paul's letter to the Philippians, I was captured with the level of passion in the heart of the Apostle for Christ and His gospel. I was not surprised, because, of course, we are looking at the life and ministry of this amazing servant of the Lord. What did surprise me, however, was that Paul did not see himself, or his level of commitment as exceptional or unusual. As he writes to shepherd this beloved church around the gospel, he assumes that his model is the norm for all who will follow Christ and give themselves to His Kingdom.

The more I read, the more I wanted to experience this normal Christian life that is modeled by the Apostle Paul. I want to know more of Christ, and the reality of His eternal Kingdom, and to live beyond the boundaries of a typical Christian lifestyle driven by our cultural expectations. I think you share the same dreams, since you chose to join me in this study.

May God be gracious to us as we look into this wonderful letter between the great apostle and this church that loved him so, and served him with every resource they had. And may God give us a double measure of the passion they shared for each other, and for the gospel of the Cross!

*I thank my God in all my remembrance of you,
always in every prayer of mine for you all making
my prayer with joy, because of your partnership
in the gospel from the first day until now.*

Philippians 1:3–5

1

The Power of Partnerships

Paul's letter to the church at Philippi is a "thank you note." You have given financial gifts to churches, friends in need, missionaries and Christian organizations. Often, in response, you have received a letter expressing their gratitude to you for your generous support and your help to them. I doubt that you have ever received a "thank you" letter on the level of Paul's letter to this wonderful church!

The Philippian church loved Paul because he brought the gospel to them and encouraged them again and again. He loved them because they consistently supported him financially in his ministry as an apostle. In fact, later in this letter, he tells them that they were the only church supporting him financially during many times in his ministry (Philippians 4:15).

> I thank my God in all my remembrance of you, always in every prayer of mine for you all making my prayer with joy, because of your partnership in the gospel from the first day until now. (Philippians 1:3–5)

The Philippian church was not a wealthy church, but they were a generous church! We know this, not only from the Philippian letter, but because as Paul was encouraging the church at Corinth to provide an offering to help the persecuted church at Jerusalem, he held up the churches of Macedonia as an example to them.

JOY THAT IS INSIDE OUT

> We want you to know, brothers, about the grace of God
> that has been given among the churches of Macedonia, for
> in a severe test of affliction, their abundance of joy and
> their extreme poverty have overflowed in a wealth of
> generosity on their part. (2 Corinthians 8:1–2)

The churches of Macedonia (Philippi's location) were also
experiencing afflictions. They, too, knew extreme poverty, but
they owned an abundance of joy! That joy gave birth to a wealth
of generosity. Even in the midst of their own needs, they begged
the Apostle Paul to allow them to participate in this relief
offering for their hurting brothers and sisters in Jerusalem.

> For they gave according to their means, as I can testify,
> and beyond their means, of their own accord, begging us
> earnestly for the favor of taking part in the relief of the
> saints—and this, not as we expected, but they gave
> themselves first to the Lord and then by the will of God to
> us. (2 Corinthians 8:3–5)

This is a strong reminder to all of us that the call of God to
give is not limited to the wealthy, or to those who have a gift of
giving. The call is to every child of God, and every gathering of
His people. How can "abundance of joy" and "extreme poverty"
fit together? Only in the presence of God and His work among
us! The joy of the Philippians that flowed from God's grace to
them, and the opportunity of being a part of what He was
doing, overflowed in their own generosity to the Jerusalem
church.

Paul referred to the joy of the Philippians in their giving,
and he tells them he is praying for them with joy. You surely
know that "joy" is one of the great themes in this Philippian
letter. As Paul writes this letter, he is either under house arrest,
as was his early experience in Rome, or he is chained between
Nero's elite guards awaiting execution, as he was in his later
days in Rome. The Philippians are in extreme poverty and the
Apostle Paul is in a Roman dungeon, yet they both experience
great joy!

When we think of the last time we overflowed with joy, we might remember a quiet evening on a beach watching a beautiful sunset with our husband, wife or best friend. Those times are great gifts from our Lord, but the joy that Paul is talking about is not a level of happiness, comfort or security that results from circumstances aligning well on our behalf. This is not a joy that comes from outside in; it comes from inside out.

This joy that enabled the Philippians to be generous when they were also in need, and moved Paul to write with such encouraging and hopeful words to those he loved, flowed from a settled confidence in God. This God was at work in them and among them, even right now in these difficult circumstances. They knew God was sovereign over their life situations, and that He would fulfill His every purpose for them. He was present with them even now, and that was the source of their joy.

OUR GOD FINISHES WHAT HE BEGINS

As Paul continues his letter, He reminds them once again of this great truth, and encourages them with one of the most powerful promises of God's Word as He keeps the hearts of His people:

> And I am sure of this, that he who began a good work in you will bring it to completion at the day of Jesus Christ. (Philippians 1:6)

We feel our hearts strengthened and filled with hope as we read these words, even as the brothers and sisters in Philippi must have experienced so many years ago! Some of us have fallen on our faces in embarrassing places in our walk with the Lord. Many of us have failed to measure up to our own expectations as men and women of God. Our weaknesses convince us that we will never get this Christian life right.

To know that God will bring to completion the work that He has begun in us through His Son is the most significant part of that "settled confidence" which gives birth to joy in our hearts. We are the work of God, and His work in us is not finished yet.

21

That work is in progress, and both the process and the goal are glorious in the eyes of our God!

> It is right for me to feel this way about you all, because I hold you in my heart, for you are all partakers with me of grace, both in my imprisonment and in the defense and confirmation of the gospel. (Philippians 1:7)

Part of the work that God was doing in the church at Philippi was seen in the love that was shared between this church and the apostle who had shepherded them with the heart of their God. In our next chapter we will focus more on the role of affections in the ministry, but even now we must see the power that bound Paul and the members of this church together. This was far more than a financial transaction. It was not built primarily on Paul's amazing gifts of church planting and leadership skills. Their hearts were deeply knit into each other's.

> For God is my witness, how I yearn for you all with the affection of Christ Jesus. (Philippians 1:8)

PARTNERSHIPS ENABLE FRUITFUL MINISTRY

The partnership between Paul and the church at Philippi went far beyond giving money. Paul's greater encouragement in that Roman prison was that they were also partnering with him in his sufferings and his chains. Even beyond that, they partnered with him in God's grace as they together defended and confirmed the gospel. They were ministry partners on every level!

The mission with which I serve, Leadership Resources International, is a pastoral training ministry. We equip pastors around the world to "teach God's Word with God's heart," so we mentor preachers, teachers and shepherds in how to study the Bible well and to teach it to their people faithfully. Both our pastor-trainers and we rejoice when they learn to preach the message of the biblical author rather than using a text to preach their message.

By God's grace, we are doing this work on every populated continent, with many thousands of pastors now trained because this is not only a work of mentoring, it is also aimed at multiplying. We are equipping national pastors to train other nationals in preaching, and in bringing the Father's heart of encouragement and hope in their shepherding.

But we do not do this work alone. How could a handful of people from Chicago go to Africa, the former Soviet Union, Asia, Europe, the South Pacific or Latin America and think that we could begin a ministry of pastoral training? We do not know pastors in these areas, much less how to find "faithful men who can teach others" (2 Timothy 2:2). So we build partnerships with other missions and churches in these areas in order to select the right pastor/trainers, and then teach them to bring effective ministry in their culture and language. We also partner with churches, individuals and foundations to supply the finances needed to make these trainings possible. We partner with churches and missions to provide teachers.

This brings us to the reality of the Body of Christ, and how our God builds His Church. Not one person has all of the gifts needed for ministry. Not one church has all the resources. Not one mission owns all of the skills. When we partner together, each contributing what God has entrusted to us, ministry becomes far more fruitful and effective than any one of us could fulfill alone.

GOD'S WORD AND HIS SPIRIT ARE THE MEANS

Why do we do this? Because we long to see the Word of God flow powerfully through every church to every nation! Our passion is the promise of the prophet Habakkuk:

For the earth will be filled with the knowledge of the glory of the Lord as the waters cover the sea. (Habakkuk 2:14)

One of our primary convictions is that God fulfills that promise through the ministry of His Word in the power of His Spirit. The church at Philippi and the believers there were given life when Paul brought the Word of God to them. We see as early in our bibles as Genesis one, that God's words are the way He fulfills His purposes. When the earth was formless and void, and the Spirit of God was hovering over the waters, God began to speak:

> And God said, "Let there be light," and there was light. (Genesis 1:3)

God spoke in the midst of the darkness, and the light began to shine! This third verse in the first chapter begins an amazing repetition. Eight times we see the phrase "and God said." Each time He speaks, life springs forth in His creation. God spoke of this same hope through the prophet Isaiah.

> For as the rain and the snow come down from heaven and do not return there but water the earth, making it bring forth and sprout, giving seed to the sower and bread to the eater, so shall my word be that goes out from my mouth; it shall not return to me empty, but it shall accomplish that which I purpose, and shall succeed in the thing for which I sent it. (Isaiah 55:10–11)

Throughout history, God has fulfilled His work through the ministry of His life-giving Word in the power of the Holy Spirit. We see this same reality in the ministry of the Lord Jesus as He testified that He only spoke the words of His Father:

> For I have not spoken on my own authority, but the Father who sent me has himself given me a commandment—what to say and what to speak. And I know that his commandment is eternal life. What I say, therefore, I say as the Father has told me. (John 12:49–50)

We see this same hope in the hearts of the apostles. On the day of Pentecost, Peter preached from three Old Testament texts. As the apostles continued to proclaim the Word of God, that Word grew until the entire known world was affected by the truth of God that brings life to people, and transforms churches and nations.

Partnerships enable this work to flourish in a way that no single church or mission could ever fulfill on its own. God has blessed us with partners who share the same convictions that the Word of God brought in the power of His Spirit are both the message and the means to ministry.

PRAYING ABOUT PRAYING

Because the affections of Paul's heart were deeply knit into his brothers and sisters in Philippi, and he was now in prison, his ministry to them in this present reality was focused on prayer. He was committed to partnering with God in the work He was doing in this great church. Paul knew he could do that through prayers of intercession.

> And it is my prayer that your love may abound more and more, with knowledge and all discernment, (Philippians 1:9)

Is that not a wonderful way to pray? May your love flourish more and more! In your relationships with one another, in your care for me and our work together in the gospel, in your heart for Christ, may love flow until it fills everything we are and all that we do. Along with that love, may God give you wisdom and understanding, to know Him, His ways and His purposes.

> so that you may approve what is excellent, and so be pure and blameless for the day of Christ, filled with the fruit of righteousness that comes through Jesus Christ, to the glory and praise of God. (Philippians 1:10–11)

Paul also asked God to enable his brothers and sisters in Philippi to affirm and pursue those things that are best, to live holy lives as they prepare for the return of their Lord, and to be filled up with all that flows from a right relationship with their God. Christ is the only resource that brings those hopes to reality and results in God being worshiped and glorified.

When we read Paul's prayer for his beloved brothers and sisters, we sense that Paul is asking God to do the very things He must desire to fulfill among them! How is it that Paul prays with such understanding? I think Paul had given much thought and even prayer as he began to intercede for this church.

Rather than assuming what God wanted to do in their midst, or simply asking God to be with them, bless them or provide what they needed, Paul spent time in God's presence with a listening heart. I believe he asked God to enable him to see this church through His eyes, and cause his heart to be sensitive to what God purposed to do in them. These were the very things Paul brought back to the Lord as he interceded for his people. Then, he wrote to them the very things he was asking God to do in them.

We see this same pattern of intercession in Paul's letters to the churches at Colossae and Ephesus. He prays so knowledgably for the people God has entrusted to him in ministry, and I believe it is because he sought the Lord in prayer, asking God to open his eyes to the needs of his people, and God's purposes for them, before he assumed what they needed, or simply asked God's blessing on them.

This is a powerful pattern for our own prayers of intercession. When we pray for our children or our parents, for His will to be done on earth as it is in heaven, for pastors and leaders, for missions and missionaries, and for those God has entrusted to us, it is good to "pray about praying." We cannot assume what they need, or what God desires, or just ask, "Please bless so and so." Pray with knowledge, with God's heart, and then write to them and tell them what you are asking God to do in and for them!

GOD'S PURPOSES ARE UNSTOPPABLE

Now, Paul gives the church at Philippi an understanding of what God is doing in this very difficult and confusing time:

> I want you to know, brothers, that what has happened to me has really served to advance the gospel, so that it has become known throughout the whole imperial guard and to all the rest that my imprisonment is for Christ. And most of the brothers, having become confident in the Lord by my imprisonment, are much more bold to speak the word without fear. (Philippians 1:12–14)

These brothers and sisters who love Paul so much, and love the gospel he is proclaiming, are having a hard time understanding Paul's imprisonment and how it is affecting the growth of the gospel. The great apostle, the primary spokesman for the gospel, the one always out there on the front lines of church planting and developing leaders has been taken out of the ministry! What is God doing? Doesn't He want the gospel to advance and for churches to grow?

If you have walked with the Lord for some years, these questions are not unfamiliar to you; surely I know them very well. We are often confused in our walk with the Lord. Why is God doing this or that? Why is He not doing what I am asking Him to do? It makes no sense that these things should hinder the work of our church or our mission!

Paul makes it very clear that God is in control of these circumstances, and he is not only content with what God is doing, but actually rejoicing in it. In fact, Paul knew that God had ordained this situation to further the work of the gospel. While Paul was in prison, others were out among the people, bringing the good news about Jesus.

When we look at the end of this letter, we see Paul's sense of humor and God's as well:

> Greet every saint in Christ Jesus. The brothers who are with me greet you. All the saints greet you, especially those of Caesar's household. (Philippians 4:21–22)

Even in Caesar's own household people were coming to Christ while Paul was in chains and others were preaching! Of course, what makes this truth so remarkable is to remember who Caesar was: none other than Nero. Nero hated this gospel; he hated Christians; he embraced his identity as the one who would erase the name of Jesus from the face of this earth. What did our God say? Nero, you are confused about your identity, because I have named you as the chairman of the committee for the evangelization of the entire Roman Empire! Nero, like Pharaoh before him (Romans 9:17) was God's tool for His purposes and His glory.

PROCLAIM CHRIST!

The Apostle Paul was a humble servant of the Lord Jesus Christ. He knew that God was doing a great work, and that He had called Paul to be a partner with Him in what He was doing, but the fulfillment of the gospel was not dependent on Paul. Others were preaching while Paul was in prison. They did not share Paul's skill, his character or his heart. But God was using them instead of Paul!

> The latter do it out of love, knowing that I am put here for the defense of the gospel. The former proclaim Christ out of selfish ambition, not sincerely but thinking to afflict me in my imprisonment. (Philippians 1:16–17)

Some of these preachers were very poor representatives of the gospel. Others had very poor motives. There were even some preachers who saw Paul's imprisonment as an opportunity to advance themselves at his expense. How did Paul handle this?

> What then? Only that in every way, whether in pretense or in truth, Christ is proclaimed, and in that I rejoice. (Philippians 1:18)

As I write these words, the great evangelist Billy Graham has just gone into the presence of the Lord he loved and served. What a gift God gave to us in this powerfully gifted man of faithfulness and integrity! When I travel around the world, I continually meet pastors who not only came to know Christ but were called to serve Him through Billy Graham's ministry.

On my first visit to Moscow, I had the privilege of preaching in the Central Baptist Church in that great city. After the morning worship, I remembered that Billy Graham had preached in that very church on his first visit to Russia as an evangelist. He had prayed for years that God would allow him to preach the gospel of Christ in this communist country!

When God did give Billy Graham that opportunity in the early 1980's, there was, of course, great interest in his trip from every level of society. And there was a very large "press corps" following him wherever he went. As we know, the press can tend to be cynical. They were continually speculating whether Billy Graham was even aware of how he was being used by the communists for their propaganda and purposes.

After Billy Graham preached that morning in the Central Baptist Church, there was a "press conference." Again, speculations and cynicism ruled the day! Doesn't Billy Graham know that the people he wanted to preach to this morning were not even allowed into the church? Doesn't he know that they filled the church with KGB agents and members of the communist party?

How did Billy Graham respond? It makes no difference whether the church is filled with peasants, party members or KGB agents. The gospel is powerful enough to change anyone's life!

Like the Apostle Paul, Billy Graham was confident in the gospel of Jesus Christ. And like Paul, he gave his life for that gospel.

WHY I LOVE THIS GOSPEL!

I know well the power of this gospel! Not only have I seen the life-giving good news of sins forgiven and the hope of eternal life transform people all around the world, I saw it as a young boy in my own life and in the life of my family.

My father was a "pagan" in every sense of the word. As far as I know, he had never come in contact with the gospel of Christ or heard of this loving God who gave His Son for us. It was long after my father had died that my son Peter was doing some research into our family background and learned that my father had grown up in an orphanage. My relationship with my father was filled with pain and lacked intimacy. To know that no one had ever taught him how to be a father gave me a needed sense of compassion toward him.

My mother was Jewish. She was completely in the dark concerning a Christian worldview, or the knowledge of a God who redeems broken people. She was the most angry, bitter person I have ever known. Her family rejected her when she married my father.

When my mom and dad were first married, they lived in an apartment on the North Side of Chicago. After some time, they bought a piece of land in the southwest suburbs, built a small house and began their family. A few years later, that house burned down.

While they were trying to rebuild their home and their dreams, my father hired a man to do the electrical work. He was a Christian. As he was working on the rewiring, he noticed that my parents had three small children. He asked my parents, "Do your children go to Sunday School?" Of course, neither of my parents knew what Sunday School was! He asked, "Do you mind if I take your children with me?"

God was breaking into my life, and the life of my family, with His sovereign grace and mercy! Just as God opened Lydia's heart to respond to Paul's message, He began a beautiful work of His grace in my parents. Eventually, through the witness of this very ordinary but faithful man, my entire family came to Christ. I had the joy of leading my father to Christ a few days before he died, and I saw transformation up close as my mother became a soft and beautiful woman of God.

God's grace toward me in the gospel continued. From about age five, I was able to go to church, Sunday School, catechism, a Christian school and youth group. While I do not believe I was actually converted until I was seventeen, it is clear that God knew me long before I knew Him! Even with the brokenness along the way and the pain of many rebellious choices, God has been bringing to completion the good work He began in me.

A PLATFORM FOR THE GOSPEL

It is clear as we read the early verses of Paul's letter to Philippi that he did not see his imprisonment as a punishment for preaching the gospel. He knew that his God was at work, sovereign over his times, places and circumstances for His purposes and His glory. Paul saw his imprisonment as a platform for preaching the gospel!

Are you aware that God has been building in your life a platform for the gospel? You and I were chosen in Christ from the foundation of the world (Ephesians 1:4). Long before we were born, God was choosing our ancestors perfectly so that we would be the person He was calling us to be. He weaved us in our mother's womb (Psalm 139:13–16). He ordained our days. Every experience, every relationship, every life situation, every success and failure, have been tools in the hands of our great God to shape and prepare us as His servants (Ephesians 2:10). Our God has prepared us for ministry, and He has prepared ministry for us!

Now, this God who has shaped and prepared us has given us a platform from which to proclaim the gospel that no one else shares. In our family, in our neighborhood, where we attend school, our friendships, our workplace, we have been given a unique platform for the gospel that has been entrusted to us!

Doesn't Paul use interesting language as he calls the church at Philippi, and you and me, to preach from this platform? He is not using words like "witnessing," or "share your faith," or "mention the name of Jesus when your family gathers." He is using bigger terms, more weighty words. He talks of "defending and confirming the gospel."

How do we defend the gospel? We proclaim the Word of God, and share our knowledge of His work in the Cross, the death of Christ for our sins, and His resurrection. We call people to repentance and faith in Him. How do we confirm the gospel? We confirm the gospel in how we handle our money, in the attitudes of our hearts as they become like those of God's own Son, as we walk with our brothers and sisters the way God calls us to walk, we confirm the gospel. We confirm the gospel in the faithfulness of our marriage, and every time we care for the poor and pursue justice and mercy in the name of Jesus.

HE WHO BEGAN HIS GOOD WORK

The verse near the beginning of this beautiful letter that we treasure so, and brings such hope to our hearts is fascinating in the context:

> And I am sure of this, that he who began a good work in you will bring it to completion at the day of Jesus Christ. (Philippians 1:6)

What is the good work that Paul is referring to here? Surely God is providing assurance for doubtful and struggling believers. He will have brought to completion His work in us when we see Christ face to face! But while we are still here, God is relentlessly continuing His work in us. He is calling us and preparing us to partner with Him in the gospel. Just as in the church at Philippi, God is orienting every resource we have, every attitude of our hearts, every relationship we share, every passion of our soul, around the gospel of His Son!

USING THE STUDY GUIDE

At the end of each chapter, you will find questions for personal reflection and group discussion. Each guide also ends with encouragements toward group and personal prayer. If you are using this book as a personal devotional tool or a means of strengthening your commitment to the gospel, we hope these questions will help to lead you in that process.

It is our strong desire, however, that you will invite your small group, home fellowship or Sunday morning class to join you in this study. Both the book and the study guide contain strong challenges to our western lifestyle in relationship to the gospel, and substantial encouragement to heart changes toward praying, giving, going and acting on the gospel. Most often, deep changes are made in the environment of group interaction and prayer.

As you prepare to use this devotional Bible study for your group, it would be best to secure a book for each participant. In preparation for your scheduled meeting, have each student read through the selected chapter and think through the questions in an attitude of prayer, coming prepared to share their own reflections and responses with the rest of the group. May God bless you richly as you share His Word and your commitment to His gospel together!

STUDY GUIDE

1. Has there been a time in your life when you experienced both joy and poverty at the same time? Perhaps it wasn't a financial poverty, but social, emotional or through physical limitations. Find the verses in Philippians that confirm this combination is possible.

2. Is it good to be generous to others in our own times of great need? Is it always financial? Find the verses in Philippians that describe the goal of giving. Then discuss what parameters there are, if any.

3. When you read that "He who began a good work in you will bring it to completion at the day of Jesus Christ," how is your heart most encouraged? Support your response from the text of Philippians.

4. Can you name three mission partnerships through which you or your church is serving to advance the gospel? How have you been strengthened through these partnerships? How has the fruit of your ministry been multiplied because you are serving together?

5. When you look at your mission outreaches, do you see clearly the relationship between God's Word and the working of His Spirit? In what way? How do these things reflect what Paul is communicating to the church in Philippi?

6. What is the significance in both our preaching and humanitarian ventures being the means by which God fulfills His work through His Word? Support your response from the text of Philippians.

7. What is Paul's model for ministering through intercessional prayer? Find the verses in Philippians that explain it to the reader. How would following his example change your prayer ministries both corporately and privately?

8. Have you ever tried to change God's mind, get Him to "sign off" on your idea or refused to do what you clearly heard Him tell you to do? How did that turn out for you? Why?

9. Using Philippians 1:15–18, discuss how our personal choices affect the message of the gospel going out.

10. Using Philippians 3:17–20, discuss how our personal choices affect only our lives.

11. What are some of the unique experiences God has used in your life to build a platform for the gospel?

12. If God is working out His purposes to orient everything that you have and everything you are around the gospel of His Son, how is that process going? In what areas do you need to grow the most for that process to be nourished?

PRAYER

Spend some time personally, or as a group, thanking God for giving you not only everything you need, but sufficient to be generous. Worship Him for His sovereignty over every purpose of His heart, and for His sovereignty over that process of building into your life a platform for the gospel. Ask God to show you how to partner with Him and with His people to bring the gospel to the nations.

For to me to live is Christ, and to die is gain.

Philippians 1:21

2

The Role of Affections in the Gospel

The relationship between the church at Philippi and the Apostle Paul was not rooted in a strategic partnership for the sake of advancing the gospel. It was not based on Paul's need for financial support and the generosity of the Macedonians who believed in his ministry. This relationship soared to the glory of God because of the deep love Paul had for his brothers and sisters in Philippi, and their love for him.

As he introduced this letter, Paul told them that he "held them in his heart." He described how he "yearned for them with all of the affection of Christ Jesus." Is Jesus actually as much about affections as He is about truth?

We are greatly challenged as we consider how Paul constructs his letter, how he focuses on relationships and hearts! We are forced to ask ourselves whether our faith is primarily a matter of the head or of the heart. Even more, we are confronted with the question: What does the gospel have to do with the affections of our heart?

AFFECTIONS AND MINISTRY TEAMS

Later in this letter, Paul talks extensively and intimately about his ministry team.

> I hope in the Lord Jesus to send Timothy to you soon, so that I too may be cheered by news of you. (Philippians 2:19)

Wait a minute! Is this a ministry reason big enough to send Timothy to Macedonia? Especially if this is a supporting church! Wouldn't it be better to say: "I am sending Timothy to preach to you, since I am not able to come, and he is the next best preacher on the team?" Is it not more reasonable to say: "Since it has been some time that we were together, Timothy will be able to see if you have strayed from the truth, or if you are continuing in doctrinal purity?" All this time, distance and money so that "I may be cheered by you?" Is that a need big enough to justify this investment?

Paul was able to be honest about his need for fellowship and encouragement in the ministry. His priority of relationships over strategic success is all over his letters. To the church at Corinth, he told of leaving an "open door" in Troas because of his need for Titus (2 Corinthians 2:12–13). He told the church at Thessalonica he was "affectionately desirous of them" (1 Thessalonians 2:8). To the church at Corinth he said "I seek not what is yours, but you!" (2 Corinthians 12:14). For Paul, heart relationships were high priority in the ministry, because those affections not only fueled the work, they knitted the team together. So he can genuinely say to his brothers and sisters, "I need to be cheered by you!"

As Paul continued to talk about Timothy, we can clearly see how he lifts his brother high in the eyes of those in Philippi. Paul talks of how pure Timothy's motives are and how genuine his concern.

> For I have no one like him, who will be genuinely concerned for your welfare. For they all seek their own interests, not those of Jesus Christ. (Philippians 2:20–21)

BRAGGING ABOUT YOUR CO-WORKERS

I think Paul liked to "brag" about his co-workers! He wanted all who read his letters to value these servants of the Lord the way he did, and to lift them high with esteem. These servants are men and women of character, and worthy of not only your respect, but your love and thanksgiving as well. In fact, Paul made it clear that his relationship with Timothy far transcended that of a colleague or a ministry co-worker. His relationship with Timothy was intimate, like family, where hearts matter more than sheer skill or competence in the work.

> But you know Timothy's proven worth, how as a son with a father he has served with me in the gospel. I hope therefore to send him just as soon as I see how it will go with me, and I trust in the Lord that shortly I myself will come also. (Philippians 2:22–24)

To understand how significant relationships of intimacy and life were to the Apostle Paul, and how important it was to him that others look upon fellow-workers with value and esteem, take a few moments and read the close of his letter to the church at Rome. Talk about gossiping about your co-workers! It is all over, around and through this warm and affectionate closing. Note, too, how important it is to Paul that we see women in ministry through the eyes of our God (they make up most of this list in Romans 16:1–16).

We know that Paul shared a special relationship with Timothy, whom he calls "his beloved child" (2 Timothy 1:2), or as we read here in Philippians, his son. But this attitude was not limited to Timothy. It was reflected in other ministry relationships as well. Epaphroditus was a messenger between Paul and the church at Philippi:

> I have thought it necessary to send to you Epaphroditus my brother and fellow worker and fellow soldier, and your messenger and minister to my need, for he has been longing for you all and has been distressed because you heard that he was ill. (Philippians 2:25–26)

OUR AFFECTIONS FOR ONE ANOTHER OVERFLOW FROM OUR AFFECTIONS FOR CHRIST

What held these relationships together and wove them deeply into the hearts of these brothers? We are looking at something here far beyond shared ministry functions, or talents and gifts coming together on a team to stimulate strategic initiatives into a successful venture. We see hearts knit deeply into one another's by the Holy Spirit, a love brought into fullness by the Christ who lives within them. They loved each another because they loved the Lord Who had called them to serve together.

I will freely confess that what I write here is colored by my experience of serving with Leadership Resources. Our team relationships are truly characterized by warmth and love; we do seek to lift one another with value and esteem. Our first level of relationship is affectionate friendships rather than functional roles.

We do not always get it right! We often fail each other. There are sins and hurts as we serve together. But we are quick to confess our sins to each other and to forgive one another. We despise competition, political environments and self-promotion. We sincerely desire to lift up our co-workers with esteem in the eyes of our fellow servants so that Christ is exalted not only in what we do, but in how we walk together in the process.

> Indeed he was ill, near to death. But God had mercy on him, and not only on him but on me also, lest I should have sorrow upon sorrow. (Philippians 2:27)

We can see clearly that Paul's heart was caught up in Epaphroditus' experience in a way that far transcends comments about a colleague's challenging situation. He loved this brother deeply, and his heart was fully invested in what Epaphroditus was experiencing now. Paul treasured his brother and needed him greatly!

> I am the more eager to send him, therefore, that you may rejoice at seeing him again, and that I may be less anxious. So receive him in the Lord with all joy, and honor such men. (Philippians 2:28–29)

CHRIST: BEGINNING, END, EVERYTHING

Returning to our context of looking at chapter one in Paul's letter, we see the full depth of Paul's model of affections and the gospel. He knew that his brothers and sisters in Philippi were praying that he would be delivered from that Roman prison and that he would be able to visit them again.

> Yes, and I will rejoice, for I know that through your prayers and the help of the Spirit of Jesus Christ this will turn out for my deliverance, (Philippians 1:18b-19)

Deliverance from those chains was Paul's desire, too, but not his highest goal. Far more than being set free from those guards, he wanted to honor His Lord. Even if it meant dying in that prison, Paul's priority was that Christ would be glorified in him.

> as it is my eager expectation and hope that I will not be at all ashamed, but that with full courage now as always Christ will be honored in my body, whether by life or by death. (Philippians 1:20)

He tells us why. Here is Paul's testimony. Christ is the beginning of his life, the end of his hopes and dreams, and the fullness of everything in between. Jesus was the satisfaction and the fulfillment of his heart's desires. So it must be for you and me. If we knew what we really wanted, we would want Christ!

> For to me to live is Christ, and to die is gain. (Philippians 1:21)

For the Apostle Paul, this was the explanation for his incredible life and ministry. Christ is the one who enabled him day by day in his relentless schedule as he served his Lord. Jesus was his motivation for his preaching and his sufferings. His satisfaction along the way, the sustaining grace every moment, and the joy of God's presence, were all found in Christ.

To die is gain? Who talks like this? Only a believer who has tasted in small measure the pleasures of knowing Christ, and who passionately desires more! We do not often think of death as gain. We seek to comfort grieving brothers and sisters in the loss of a loved one. At the same time, we need to remind them, and ourselves, death means loss for those left behind, but gain for the one in the presence of the Lord.

> If I am to live in the flesh, that means fruitful labor for me. Yet which I shall choose I cannot tell. I am hard pressed between the two. My desire is to depart and be with Christ, for that is far better. But to remain in the flesh is more necessary on your account. (Philippians 1:22–24)

I learned this in a new way a few years ago when I underwent surgery and chemotherapy treatments for cancer. I love my wife Karen and treasure every moment I can spend with her. The thought of dying and leaving her did not seem to be a "gain" in my eyes. Facing life's realities, I do remember saying to her "but 100 more years with you would still not be enough"! Karen, without question, is God's most precious gift to me, in the gift of His Son.

My struggle in this area is driven deeper because of my love for this world. The Apostle John had warned us: "Do not love this world or the things in the world" (1 John 2:15). I must confess, I love this world far too much! I am not referring to the desires of the flesh, the desires of eyes or the pride of life (although I have had sufficient battles with those as well). I am talking about the life God has given me in this world. I love my wife, I love my sons, I love my work, I love my sports and hobbies. I have asked Karen to pray with me that my love for this world would diminish, and I would look more and more toward heaven as gain.

DESIRES, LONGINGS AND GROANINGS

I remember in these earthly battles how I turned Paul's words completely around. I said to Karen: "I am willing to go and to be with the Lord, but I want to stay here with you!" Paul was willing to stay here for the sake of the Philippians, but he wanted to go home, into the presence of his beloved Lord.

> Convinced of this, I know that I will remain and continue with you all, for your progress and joy in the faith, so that

in me you may have ample cause to glory in Christ Jesus, because of my coming to you again. (Philippians 2:25–26)

Paul's sharing with the church at Philippi of his desire to be with Christ is not the only time he talked of this reality. As he wrote to the church at Corinth about these same desires, he described his feelings of "groaning and longing" while in this earthly body:

For in this tent we groan, longing to put on our heavenly dwelling, if indeed by putting it on we may not be found naked. (2 Corinthians 5:2–3)

Like Paul, we groan because when we receive Christ, we become a new creation in Him, and are now an eternal person. But we still live in a body designed for this world. We begin to long for the eternal body fit for a new creation that we will receive in the resurrection. In the meantime we groan because even in a temporal world we have become hungry for eternal realities! We begin to "long" for more and more of eternity, and release from the restraints of time, the physical world, and this body that has not been redeemed from sin.

For while we are still in this tent, we groan, being burdened—not that we would be unclothed, but that we would be further clothed, so that what is mortal may be swallowed up by life. He who has prepared us for this very thing is God, who has given us the Spirit as a guarantee. (2 Corinthians 5:4–5)

Isn't that a beautiful description of our experience in the resurrection and the transformation that will take place when we receive our "eternal dwelling"? Everything of this world, even death itself will be "swallowed up," overwhelmed, overtaken, by life itself! So we can be sure that our Father will follow through with His eternal promises. He has given us a "down payment" of all that we will share in with Him forever: the Holy Spirit, the very power and presence of Christ living in us right now.

HOME IS WHERE OUR HEARTS LONG TO BE

> So we are always of good courage. We know that while we are at home in the body we are away from the Lord, for we walk by faith, not by sight. Yes, we are of good courage, and we would rather be away from the body and at home with the Lord. (2 Corinthians 5:6–8)

Absent from the body, home with the Lord! Isn't home the warmest and most inviting description of heaven we find in our Bibles? Sometimes, when we experience the death of a loved one in our family, and we try to explain to children what has just happened, we might say: "Grandmother has gone on a journey, and someday we will see her again." But in reality, this world and the realm of time are the journey; home is the destination.

Home is always the place where we are most comfortable. Everything there belongs to us. It is all in the right place. Even on our most wonderful travel holidays, with all of the joys along the way, the place where our hearts most long to be is home! Our Father is preparing a home for us in heaven. Our hearts will finally be settled in that place; everything will be just right, and the Lord we have loved will be there with us.

> So whether we are at home or away, we make it our aim to please him. (2 Corinthians 5:9)

To both the church at Corinth and the church at Philippi, Paul told of his willingness to remain here, but his desire was to depart, and to be with Christ. He well knew that this was all a matter of God's sovereign timing, and he was free to let that rest in His hands. What mattered most to Paul, however, was his desire to please his master.

AFFECTIONS, PASSIONS AND FUEL FOR THE GOSPEL

What was the driving force behind Paul's ministry? He worked tirelessly, endlessly, with every resource, physically, emotionally and spiritually. Surely, he was called by Christ on the Damascus road and commissioned as an apostle. Paul clearly saw his work as an eternal stewardship that had been entrusted to him. He continually referred to himself as a bondservant of Christ. But it was his desire to please his Lord that moved him the most. Paul loved Jesus, and desired with all of his heart to bring Him pleasure!

Why was death a "gain" for Paul? Because what had happened to him on that Damascus road was more than just a "conversion"! Yes, he was born again that day when he believed that Jesus was the risen Christ. He was changed from being a very religious Pharisee to a follower of the Messiah. On the deepest level, however, a growing relationship of love was begun that very day between the Apostle Paul and the Lord Jesus.

That is why Paul longed to be released from his earthly body, and to be with Jesus in heaven. The longer he walked with Christ, the more he saw the beautiful heart of his Lord, the more he loved Him and desired His presence. This physical world separated Paul from the One he loved the most, and Paul wanted every barrier to the fullness of love, fellowship and joy with his Lord removed.

Paul was passionate about the gospel because he was passionate about Jesus! He was not driven in ministry primarily by the need of men and women to be saved; he was driven by his desire to please Christ. Because this gospel bore the name of Jesus, the one he loved the most, Paul gave his life for that gospel. The passions of Paul's soul had become enflamed toward Christ, and that love empowered and moved him to bring the gospel to the ends of the earth.

ONLY THE LOVE OF CHRIST CAN COMPEL US

We are well aware of the difficulty we face in our churches as we seek to move our people to the gospel. How can we motivate them to share their faith, to give to missions and to go anywhere for the good news of God's love for this world in His Son? How do we move them to pray for missionaries, for the growth of the gospel in hurting places, or for God's righteousness and justice to reign in this hurting world? I have often thought that if we want to make sure that we will have the smallest gathering of people in our church over the entire calendar year, all we need to do is plan a prayer meeting for missions. We can be sure only a handful of people will show up!

Why do we struggle so as we seek to move our people to the gospel? Where is the battle? Is the problem that our people do not know how to share their faith very well, and so they feel inadequate? Do we need better programs for evangelism and missions? Do we need to restructure the church priorities so that evangelism and care for the poor becomes more of a focus?

I am all for programs and priorities that help us to become more effective in the work of the gospel. Let's take advantage of everything the church around the world is learning so that we all can be even more fruitful. But the warfare within our people is deeper than better programs and higher priorities can solve. The truth is that we will never be passionate about the gospel unless we are passionate about Jesus!

> All this is from God, who through Christ reconciled us to himself and gave us the ministry of reconciliation; that is, in Christ God was reconciling the world to himself, not counting their trespasses against them, and entrusting to us the message of reconciliation. Therefore, we are ambassadors for Christ, God making his appeal through us. We implore you on behalf of Christ, be reconciled to God. (2 Corinthians 5:18–20)

God has committed to us the ministry of reconciliation. We are His ambassadors as we bring hope to a very dark world. This is incredible news! We had rebelled against Him, and along with Adam and Eve declared our independence from Him, and now God has reconciled us to Himself through the death of His Son. He has also called us to partner with Him in carrying that gospel to the world, using that unique platform He has designed in us to proclaim the message of His grace.

In this great text in his letter to the church at Corinth, Paul not only reveals to us our call in the gospel, he tells us how God moves us to give ourselves for that gospel.

> For the love of Christ controls us, because we have concluded this: that one has died for all, therefore all have died; (2 Corinthians 5:14)

The love of Christ compels us to the ministry of reconciliation! Nothing less than God's love for us in His Son, and our response love to Him will move us. Not better programs, not pressure, not guilt, not fear, nor any manipulations of the flesh are powerful enough to get us involved in missions or evangelism. Only the love of Christ, and our gratitude for His marvelous grace, will move us.

SEEING THROUGH THE EYES OF GOD

> he died for all, that those who live might no longer live for themselves but for him who for their sake died and was raised. (2 Corinthians 5:15)

Our passions and priorities are transformed when we are compelled by the love of Christ. Paul describes here a turning point in our life experience as God gets hold of our hearts. We used to live for ourselves just like most people around us. But how could we continue to live like that when He gave His life for us? The only reasonable and normal response is that we stop living for ourselves, and now live only for Him!

> From now on, therefore, we regard no one according to the flesh. Even though we once regarded Christ according to the flesh, we regard him thus no longer. Therefore, if anyone is in Christ, he is a new creation. The old has passed away; behold, the new has come. (2 Corinthians 5:16–17)

Another incredibly transforming experience is ours when Christ's love compels us. God gives us the grace to see people through His eyes! We have learned to see people "according to the flesh" in our walk through this world. We measure their value by outward things like color, money, education or positions of power and control. We have learned to see people in light of how we can benefit from them or use them for our purposes. But everything has changed! Now we see a person's value rooted in God's image that they bear, and their worth found only in the Father's eyes. Those who are oppressed in this world become more and more valuable in our eyes. We look at everyone now in light of who they will become in Christ as a new creation!

Paul tells us "all of this is from God." Only He can change the hearts of people and transform us on this level. Only God can turn self-centered believers' hearts to Himself rather than continuing the old patterns of consuming our lives on ourselves. Only God can give life to dead people in His new creation.

The new creation, transformed lives and the ministry of reconciliation fulfilled—all of this is from God! He is at work, filling the earth with the knowledge of His glory, preparing the throne room to be filled with those from every tribe, tongue, people and nation! And God has called you and me to be a part of that great eternal work.

How do we get there? Only the love of Christ can move us to lay down our lives for the gospel. Like the Apostle Paul, we will only become passionate about the gospel when we become passionate about Jesus! Like Paul, nothing less than our soul's passions enflamed toward the One who loved us and gave Himself for us can fuel our walk with God in missions and evangelism.

SUFFERING AND THE GOSPEL

As Paul comes to the close of this first chapter in his letter, he reminds his brothers and sisters in Philippi that his imprisonment and his chains are not unique for those who bring the good news of Christ. Every one of God's children experiences the afflictions of this world. We do this, in part, because sufferings are a major aspect of God's call to us in Christ.

> For it has been granted to you that for the sake of Christ you should not only believe in him but also suffer for his sake, engaged in the same conflict that you saw I had and now hear that I still have. (Philippians 1:29–30)

We have two callings in Christ Jesus: one is to believe, and the other is to suffer for His sake. God has designed ministry in such a way that the gospel is carried to the world through the sufferings of His people. It has been this way for all of history, and it is just as true for us today.

There are many preachers available to us today who proclaim another gospel. Paul referred to them as "peddlers of God's word" (2 Corinthians 2:17). In order to gain followers after themselves, they turn the gospel around. God has made it clear that in this world, even with the joys along the way, we will face persecution and suffering.

> Indeed, all who desire to live a godly life in Christ Jesus will be persecuted, (2 Timothy 3:12)

We can be sure, if we are a follower of Christ, that His cross will touch our lives at some time, in some way. We will remember how Jesus said as He called His disciples:

> And calling the crowd to him with his disciples, he said to them, "If anyone would come after me, let him deny himself and take up his cross and follow me." (Mark 8:34)

The glory is yet to come, when we are with the Lord. But for the sake of money and fame, many preachers will change the gospel. They will preach: "Glory now! God lives to keep you healthy, to make you wealthy, to bring you happiness!" This message, so attractive to the flesh, is painfully popular in this world, But it is a terrible lie, designed for a "make believe world."

Why is this message so popular? It does two things very effectively: it makes pastors very rich, and it gives hurting people a false hope for a better life. It also brings great shame to the name of Jesus. God tells us the truth about carrying the gospel to a world filled with pain and persecutions. The sufferings of this world will touch us deeply and cost us our lives. It is His call, and His way.

BECAUSE HE IS WORTH IT

When I think of suffering and the gospel, I remember Pastor Tham. I wanted to attend our first pastoral training in one of the mountainous countries of Asia, but my schedule did not permit me to go. However, my friend and co-worker, Craig, President of Leadership Resources, was able to participate. On the first morning of their meetings, one pastor who had registered for the training had not yet arrived. As Craig was waiting to begin, he saw a man walking toward the meeting place, and he wondered if this might be the pastor they were all waiting for. He was, and that was how Craig met Pastor Tham.

Pastor Tham was very quiet that first day the pastors met together, and hardly entered into the group discussions around the biblical texts they were studying. Finally, when Craig had the opportunity to talk with him through an interpreter, Pastor Tham told him that this very week he had decided to leave the ministry. He had a large family, and the costs for educating children in his country were very high. Some of his children were close to attending university. His church could not pay him very much, and his ministry included travel to encourage other pastors. The church was not able to help much with those expenses either. Much of those costs came out of the family funds.

Pastor Tham told Craig that he had finally decided that he needed to quit the ministry and get a job to support his family. He had already signed up for this training, however, and decided to attend before he resigned his church. That week, the group was studying the book of Jonah. How Pastor Tham wrestled with that message; how he battled with the Lord! Finally, he told Craig: "How can I be another reluctant prophet? How can I run away from God?"

I was able to join another training in this country and to meet Pastor Tham about two years later. Nothing had changed in his finances or his family situation. He was still seeking God's provision for the needs of his family and trusting Him along the way. An important part of our pastoral training times include reports from the pastor trainers of their second-generation training. As I mentioned earlier, we are equipping national pastors to train other nationals in preaching and shepherding.

When it came time for Pastor Tham to give his report, he told us how he walked four days, fourteen hours a day, over the foothills of the Himalayas to reach his second-generation team. I was so overwhelmed with what I was hearing that I could not speak for the rest of the evening! Our difficulty in these situations is not so much that we feel unworthy to be teachers of servants such as these—we often feel unworthy to even be in the same room with them.

I was so moved by Pastor Tham's report. I struggled through an almost sleepless night, praying for him and countless other precious brothers and sisters in similar circumstances around the world. The next morning, however, I had the opportunity to express my appreciation and gratitude to him. He, of course, had difficulty understanding why I was so moved by what he had shared; this was his normal service to his Lord. Then I asked him: "Why would you do this?" He said only one thing in response: "Because He is worth it!"

Like Pastor Tham and the Apostle Paul, only when the passions of our soul are enflamed in our love for Christ will we be moved to lay down our lives for the gospel.

STUDY GUIDE

1. What evidence do you see in the text of Philippians, leading up to Philippians 2:19, that Paul needs encouragement? Is it reasonable for Paul to be asking a ministry partner to travel to get and give in person messages for the sake of his encouragement? From the text, what causes us to need encouragement? How are we to work together to fulfill that need?

2. Using the text, name the ways Paul "brags" about his co-workers. Match up the compliments Paul is giving his co-workers with the exhortations and encouragements he is giving the church of Philippi in chapter one and the beginning of chapter two. What hinders or nurtures that kind of relationship among you?

3. Do you agree that our affections for one another overflow from our affections for the Lord Jesus? Support your answer from the text of Philippians.

4. Put in your own words what it means to you that "For to me to live is Christ." Support it from the text of chapter one.

5. Do you, as Bill described in his own life, struggle with loving this world too much? Are you ready to say "to die is gain" let alone say it with a whole heart? Where does the desire for this life show up in your life? What is the cause of it? Support this last answer from the text of Philippians.

6. Be honest with yourself, you don't have to share everything with the group. Take a moment to write down the deep longings of your soul. What are the things that you long for? What motivates these longings? Are you able to relate to Paul's experience of longing to be with Christ; how much or how little? Does the thought of growing the desire to be with Christ intimidate or frighten you? Would it be worth it to prioritize Christ above the needs and joys of family, friends, and career to the point that we really are torn, as Paul was, over which was better? What sacrifices would you need to make in order for that to happen?

7. When we looked at the progression in 2 Corinthians 5:14–21 in light of how God moves us to the ministry of reconciliation, is there any part of that process that is lacking in your experience? Pair up and using the text explain the steps to each other and how they have been

52

manifested in your life. If one of them hasn't, that's OK; now is the time to incorporate it and learn to live it. Which makes these other things we've been discussing all the more important!

8. Find the verses in Philippians where we see evidence that "Paul was passionate about the gospel because he was passionate about Jesus"? Pair up again and compare your answer(s) to this question with the question seven 2 Corinthians 5 text. What are the implications of that reality in our churches and in our personal lives?

9. Where has the call to "suffer for His sake" touched your life? Are you able to see this as a normal part of following Jesus? When the cross touches your life in this way, do you tend to respond with resentment or with joy?

10. Pastor Tham explained his willingness to suffer by saying: "He is worth it!" How does Paul describe the worthiness of Jesus in his letter to the Philippians? Support your answer from the text. How does this match your response in times of want, pressure, pain, loss and persecution? What is the point of changing and/or growing in this aspect of our faith? Support your answer from the text.

PRAYER

As you come to the conclusion of studying this chapter, reflect on the nature of your relationships in ministry. Ask God to give you His heart for one another, and the responses that would draw the world to see the genuineness of your faith in your love for each other. Pray that God would enflame the affections of your soul toward Him, so that you would be passionate about the gospel entrusted to you. Worship the God who loved you first, so that you can love your brothers and sisters, to love Him in return, and love the gospel that bears the name of His beloved Son!

And being found in human form, he humbled himself by becoming obedient to the point of death, even death on a cross.

Philippians 2:8

3

A God Exalted in His Humility

How do we walk worthy of this glorious gospel that has been entrusted to us? The Apostle Paul makes clear in his letter to the church at Philippi that this "worthy walk" is seen in the attitudes of our hearts and our relationships with one another as we walk together in our church.

> Only let your manner of life be worthy of the gospel of Christ, so that whether I come and see you or am absent, I may hear of you that you are standing firm in one spirit, with one mind striving side by side for the faith of the gospel, (Philippians 1:27)

Because we are in Christ and He has given us His Holy Spirit, we share an unbreakable bond of unity with our brothers and sisters in the Body of our Lord. The glue that binds us together in Christ enables us to stand firm even when the mindset of this system would woo us away from our calling, or the enemies of the gospel threaten our safety, security, or the ministry of reconciliation that God has given to us.

Since we share the same way of thinking, our hearts remain focused on Christ and His Kingdom. Our call to the gospel and the powerful "Yes" in the commitments of our hearts in response to that call enable us to not only stand firm, but to strive together for the faith passed down to us from the men and women who have given their lives so that we can partake together in the hope of this gospel.

> For it has been granted to you that for the sake of Christ you should not only believe in him but also suffer for his sake, (Philippians 1:29)

STAND, STRIVE, NO FEAR

I am curious as I watch brothers and sisters, even church leaders, respond to the increasing threats of political systems, or even our own culture, so set against this gospel. Those of us who believe in the Word of God and place our faith in the death and resurrection of Christ for our sins, face increasing ridicule in this world. We are often seen as mindless, even heartless, very small and rigid people.

Of course, the gospel makes us the largest, most loving, embracing and compassionate of all people! As our Lord gives us His heart, we are quick to place our arms around those who are poor and oppressed, broken, fallen, sick and sinful. We know our own failures and sin, and we know the God who brings mercy, forgiveness and healing to our lives. Now we invade the darkness around us confidently, proclaiming this message of life and hope, knowing that our God's love and truth will triumph over this dying system. We remember well Paul's words concerning his own imprisonment:

> I want you to know, brothers, that what has happened to me has really served to advance the gospel, so that it has become known throughout the whole imperial guard and to all the rest that my imprisonment is for Christ. And most of the brothers, having become confident in the Lord by my imprisonment, are much more bold to speak the word without fear. (Philippians 1:12–14)

Why should we feel threatened or fearful when the tongues of the arrogant strut through the earth (Psalm 73:9)? Have we not read the end of the Book? We know that when time merges with eternity once again, every purpose of our Father's heart will be fulfilled, the earth will be filled with the knowledge of the glory of the Lord as the waters cover the sea (Habakkuk 2:14) and the throne room will be filled with those from every tribe, tongue, people and nation worshiping our glorious Lord forever!

When I think of Paul's exhortation to "not be frightened by your opponents," I remember reading a fascinating story in a biography of Watchman Nee, the great Bible teacher in China during the early to Mid-Twentieth Century. Angus Kinnear tells of a meeting between Chou En-Lai and the leaders of the Christian church in China.

> In his night-long meeting with the founders of the Chinese Christian Three Self Patriotic Movement, Prime Minister Chou En-Lai made clear the Party's position on freedom of Christian witness. "We are going to let you go on trying to convert people, provided you also continue your social services. After all, we both believe that truth will prevail. We think your beliefs untrue and false; therefore if we are right, the people will reject them and your church will decay. If you are right, then the people will believe you; but as we are sure that you are wrong, we are prepared for that risk."[1]

Prime Minister Chou En-Lai made a very bad bet that night. What has happened since that late-night meeting? Communism has decayed and the church of the Lord Jesus has flourished in China! We are witnessing one of the greatest revivals in history in that great nation; in fact, there may very well be more believers in China than any other country in the world.

Stand firm; strive side by side; don't be frightened by your opponents! How did Paul carry the church in Philippi, and how does God bring us as a church to the place where we can walk like this, in a manner worthy of the gospel? This is where he points us directly to our example, the Lord Jesus Christ.

---

[1] Angus I. Kinnear, *Against The Tide: The Story of Watchman Nee* (Fort Washington, Pennsylvania: Christian Literature Crusade, 1973), 178.

TRANSFORMED HEARTS;
TRANSFORMED RELATIONSHIPS

The Apostle Paul now calls the church at Philippi to own deeply in their life together those things for which we all hunger in our relationships with one another:

> So if there is any encouragement in Christ, any comfort from love, any participation in the Spirit, any affection and sympathy, (Philippians 2:1)

How we all long for encouragement, comfort, love, fellowship, affection and compassion! This is the nurturing, secure, life-giving environment in which God's people flourish and grow to maturity. Now, Paul says, if those are the very things you desire to flow through the relationships in your church, you also must know that they spring from these realities:

> complete my joy by being of the same mind, having the same love, being in full accord and of one mind. (Philippians 2:2)

Before we can share together those heart-healing realities described in verse one, Paul says, you must share together a common mindset, a common love commitment to each other, and we all must be moving in the same direction. Then, he reminds the church at Philippi that all of this flows from a heart attitude that must reside deeply in every believer.

> Do nothing from selfish ambition or conceit, but in humility count others more significant than yourselves. Let each of you look not only to his own interests, but also to the interests of others. (Philippians 2:3–4)

What is this attitude? Seeing others as more important than ourselves! It is the same response of heart that Paul described to the church at Rome when he said "outdo one another in showing honor" (Romans 12:10). Is it actually possible in this world to look at a brother or sister as more important than we are? Or to prefer another person to ourselves? Is Paul describing an ideal world? No, he is telling us of the new creation in Christ that we are becoming, and the new Kingdom in which we live. Paul is describing the normal Christian life.

GRASPING AND GIVING

This new attitude that transforms hearts and relationships is the very attitude of the Lord Jesus:

> Have this mind among yourselves, which is yours in Christ Jesus, who, though he was in the form of God, did not count equality with God a thing to be grasped, but emptied himself, by taking the form of a servant, being born in the likeness of men. (Philippians 2:5–7)

Jesus, very God, in the presence of the Father, owning the worship of the angels and the glories of eternity, did not hold tightly to those things that were rightfully His. He emptied Himself, not of His deity, but His eternal prerogatives and privileges, and was born as a man.

We know well about "grasping." Jesus did not grasp, but grasping is often the very story of our lives. Because we were in Adam when he sinned and when he died, we inherit both his rebellion against God and his death. We come into this world as empty people, and we spend our lives grasping to be filled. We grasp at things, experiences, success, relationships, pleasures and powers. Whatever we think will fill up and quench the gnawing emptiness of our souls, we grasp onto with the hopes of satisfaction. Jesus came into the world full, and chose to be emptied!

> And being found in human form, he humbled himself by becoming obedient to the point of death, even death on a cross. (Philippians 2:8)

Jesus did not come as any man; he did not appear as a king or a ruler. He came as the lowest form of man, a servant. He did not give Himself to any form of death; He did not die as a hero. Christ died the lowest death, that of a common criminal. He willingly gave Himself to His Father, and for you and me.

> Therefore God has highly exalted him and bestowed on him the name that is above every name, so that at the name of Jesus every knee should bow, in heaven and on earth and under the earth, and every tongue confess that Jesus Christ is Lord, to the glory of God the Father. (Philippians 2:9–11)

Since Jesus was willing to come as the lowest form of man and die the lowest form of death, God has given Him the highest place, and the highest name! Someday, every knee will bow before Him—those in heaven, those on the earth, and even those under the earth. Someday, all of God's angels of light, every person who has ever lived, and even Satan and his hosts will fall before Jesus Christ and recognize His Lordship. And today, God has given you and me the privilege and joy of worshiping the One we will exalt forever!

It is critical for us to understand that we cannot live out by means of any human resource the attitudes that Paul is calling us to embrace in these scriptures, and those that follow in this letter. Only because God is giving us both the desire and the power can we live in a way that brings joy to one another and glory to our Lord.

> Therefore, my beloved, as you have always obeyed, so now, not only as in my presence but much more in my absence, work out your own salvation with fear and trembling, for it is God who works in you, both to will and to work for his good pleasure. (Philippians 2:12–13)

WHO OWNS THE WORSHIP OF THE NATIONS?

Paul is answering here one of the biggest questions of our Bibles: who will own the worship of the nations? This question is as old as the temptation of Eve and the fall of humankind, when Satan sought the glory that belongs to God alone, and Adam and Eve desired to become gods themselves. We see the passion for self-worship on a corporate level at the tower of Babel.

> Now the whole earth had one language and the same words. And as people migrated from the east, they found a plain in the land of Shinar and settled there. And they said to one another, "Come, let us make bricks, and burn them thoroughly." And they had brick for stone, and bitumen for mortar. (Genesis 11:1–3)

Human depravity had been described vividly by our God just a few chapters earlier, before the great flood, when He said of those on the earth: "Every intention of the thoughts of his heart was only evil continually" (Genesis 6:5). Now, as the men and women of the earth begin to build their tower, the depravity is dressed up a bit, but, in fact, it is just as deep and just as ugly.

> Then they said, "Come, let us build ourselves a city and a tower with its top in the heavens, and let us make a name for ourselves, lest we be dispersed over the face of the whole earth." (Genesis 11:4)

We do not know how high they were able to build this tower, but we do know that God had to come down just to see it. But this is what depravity looks like: "Let's worship what comes from us; let's make a name for ourselves!" In response to the human passion to worship themselves and what they build, God dispersed them, and confused their languages.

Many centuries later, King Nebuchadnezzar of Babylon was consumed by the same passion as those at the tower of Babel. He built an image of gold that was ninety feet tall (thirty meters) and called everyone in his domain to worship it. His officials called all who dwelt in this great kingdom to come to the dedication of the image.

> And the herald proclaimed aloud, "You are commanded, O peoples, nations, and languages, that when you hear the sound of the horn, pipe, lyre, trigon, harp, bagpipe, and every kind of music, you are to fall down and worship the golden image that King Nebuchadnezzar has set up. And

whoever does not fall down and worship shall immediately
be cast into a burning fiery furnace." (Daniel 3:4–6)

Nebuchadnezzar's kingdom was so extensive that the call
went out to all "peoples, nations and languages." Everyone
must bow, or face the fiery furnace.

We could draw many applications from the king's call for all
people to bow before the image that he had built. Surely, this
world is calling us continually to yield to those things that are
held in great esteem and highly valued here, to worship its
gods. The main point here, however, is that this is the very
same place as the tower of Babel; this is the land of Shinar. But
we see the same human heart, the same depravity that calls us
to worship ourselves and what comes from us.

WHO IS THE GOD WHO WILL DELIVER YOU?

There were three exiles from Judah who had been taken into
captivity in Babylon. They had committed themselves to the
worship of the one true God, and they refused to bow down and
worship the image Nebuchadnezzar had made. The king was
enraged, but gave them one more opportunity to submit to him.
When they heard the "call to worship" of the instruments, they
must bow down, or face the king's terrible furnace.

> Now if you are ready when you hear the sound of the horn,
> pipe, lyre, trigon, harp, bagpipe, and every kind of music,
> to fall down and worship the image that I have made, well
> and good. But if you do not worship, you shall immediately
> be cast into a burning fiery furnace. And who is the god
> who will deliver you out of my hands? (Daniel 3:15)

What a question: "Who is the god who will deliver you out of
my hands?" Nebuchadnezzar would actually receive the answer
to his question! The brothers from Judah, however, were
unmoved.

> Shadrach, Meshach, and Abednego answered and said to
> the king, "O Nebuchadnezzar, we have no need to answer
> you in this matter." (Daniel 3:16)

We can visualize the scene. Three slaves standing before the most powerful man in the most powerful kingdom in this world, and how do they respond to his threats? "We have no need to answer you!" Why?

> If this be so, our God whom we serve is able to deliver us from the burning fiery furnace, and he will deliver us out of your hand, O king. But if not, be it known to you, O king, that we will not serve your gods or worship the golden image that you have set up. (Daniel 3:17–18)

Now the king was filled with fury! The furnace was heated seven times beyond its normal temperature. It was so hot that the soldiers who threw Shadrach, Meshach and Abednego into the furnace were consumed in the flames. When the brothers were in the fire, the king was astonished:

> Then King Nebuchadnezzar was astonished and rose up in haste. He declared to his counselors, "Did we not cast three men bound into the fire?" They answered and said to the king, "True, O king." He answered and said, "But I see four men unbound, walking in the midst of the fire, and they are not hurt; and the appearance of the fourth is like a son of the gods." (Daniel 3:24–25)

Four men, unbound, walking in the flames, and the fourth was like "a son of the gods." Who is the God who would deliver these faithful brothers from the threats of the king? The preincarnate Christ was in that furnace with Shadrach, Meshach and Abednego!

> King Nebuchadnezzar to all peoples, nations, and languages, that dwell in all the earth: Peace be multiplied to you! It has seemed good to me to show the signs and wonders that the Most High God has done for me. (Daniel 4:1–2)

Now, King Nebuchadnezzar had a completely different response to the God of Israel. He had built a very high image, but now he had met the Most High God! Nebuchadnezzar's kingdom was great in its wealth and power, but it would surely fade into history. Nebuchadnezzar had met the God whose kingdom was even greater and would last forever.

> How great are his signs, how mighty his wonders! His kingdom is an everlasting kingdom, and his dominion endures from generation to generation. (Daniel 4:3)

THE ANCIENT OF DAYS AND THE SON OF MAN

While we are in the book of Daniel, there is more of Jesus we must see here. Later in the prophet's visions, he records this amazing scene in the heavenlies:

> As I looked, thrones were placed, and the Ancient of Days took his seat; his clothing was white as snow, and the hair of his head like pure wool; his throne was fiery flames; its wheels were burning fire. A stream of fire issued and came out from before him; a thousand thousands served him, and ten thousand times ten thousand stood before him; the court sat in judgment, and the books were opened. (Daniel 7:9–10)

How could Daniel even express in human words what he saw when the heavens were opened, and he saw our God was seated on His throne? It is no wonder that later on in this chapter, he tells his people that he was "greatly alarmed" as God was revealing these eternal realities to him.

> I saw in the night visions, and behold, with the clouds of heaven there came one like a son of man, and he came to the Ancient of Days and was presented before him. And to him was given dominion and glory and a kingdom, that all peoples, nations, and languages should serve him; his dominion is an everlasting dominion, which shall not pass away, and his kingdom one that shall not be destroyed. (Daniel 7:13–14)

I remember one evening I was listening to a popular radio interview program on one of the most powerful stations in our area. The host was a professor of social psychology from the University of Chicago, and this particular evening, his guests were two theologians who were trying to make the case that Jesus never claimed to be God. In fact, they said, Jesus's favorite reference to Himself in the gospels is "Son of Man," not "Son of God." He so identified with His humanity, and that is how He desired to be known.

When Christ referred to Himself as the "Son of Man," the scribes, the Pharisees and other religious leaders were not thinking about how wonderful it was that He identified with His humanity. They knew that Jesus was claiming to be the fulfillment of this great prophesy in Daniel chapter seven! He is the God who will own the worship of all nations, peoples and languages forever. That was why they hated Him so, and purposed to put Him to death.

This is the Jesus who humbled Himself, as Paul so beautifully, gloriously described to us in Philippians chapter two! The God of creation and the Lord of glory, the One before whom every knee will bow, humbled Himself by becoming the lowest form of man, and dying the lowest form of death.

I will never forget a visit with our son Peter shortly after he began university studies. Karen and I had just helped him move into his dorm a few weeks earlier. Peter had promised us that he would join one of the Christian student groups on campus, and he still serves with InterVarsity Christian Fellowship. As we walked down the hall to his room, a poster caught my eye:

> History is filled with the record of men who would be gods,
> But only one God who would be man

No One Would Invent This Gospel

This is our God, One who exalts Himself in His humility. Of course, this is not the first time in our Bibles that the humility of our God is seen! When Adam and Eve fell in their sin, their first response was to hide from one another by means of their "loincloths." Their second response was to hide from God among the trees of the garden.

> And they heard the sound of the LORD God walking in the garden in the cool of the day, and the man and his wife hid

themselves from the presence of the LORD God among the trees of the garden. But the LORD God called to the man and said to him, "Where are you?" (Genesis 3:8–9)

This is the turning point in all of human history! We will never know what moved our God to seek Adam and Eve, and us, in our sin and hiding. Think for a moment what you would have said to Adam if you were in God's place. How long would it have taken for us to say: "You knew the consequences. You made your choices, now you need to live with them!"

And he said, "I heard the sound of you in the garden, and I was afraid, because I was naked, and I hid myself." (Genesis 3:10)

Adam and Eve had become overwhelmed and immobilized in their death. They were so consumed by their guilt, their fear and their shame that if God had not sought them that day, they would have never pursued Him. They, and we, would have spent all of time and eternity "hiding in the trees," without life and without hope.

Even into eternity, we will never understand what moved our God to humble Himself that day. Surely, He could have said: "I was right; they were wrong. They should come to me!" But He knew we would never come. Somehow, God's mercy overwhelmed His justice that day, and He brought the hope of redemption to Adam and Eve, and to you and me.

I will put enmity between you and the woman, and between your offspring and her offspring; he shall bruise your head, and you shall bruise his heel. (Genesis 3:15)

When God cursed our great enemy, He promised our Redeemer at the very same moment. The offspring of the serpent is Satan; the offspring of the woman is the Lord Jesus. At the cross, Satan bruised the heel of Jesus, and Jesus crushed his head.

What kind of God is this? A God whose most surprising attribute is humility? We expect our God to be holy, all knowing, all-powerful, glorious and sovereign over all. We do not expect Him to be humble. It just does not fit!

But our God glorifies Himself in His humility. He humbled Himself when He pursued us in our sin. He humbled Himself by giving His own Son for the lives of His enemies (Romans 5:6–11). Jesus humbled Himself by coming as the lowest form of humankind and dying the lowest form of death.

Perhaps the most beautiful invitation found in the gospels reveals the beauty of our Lord's heart, seen in the humility that far surpasses our understanding.

> Come to me, all who labor and are heavy laden, and I will give you rest. Take my yoke upon you, and learn from me, for I am gentle and lowly in heart, and you will find rest for your souls. For my yoke is easy, and my burden is light. (Matthew 11:28–30)

Now we know why no one would ever invent the gospel. We can understand why every religion in history has developed and grown. Our human passion to please or appease a deity, to gain its approval or avoid its wrath, has driven us to one religious experience after another. But no one would ever invent Christianity because no one would ever create a humble God!

The gospel must be revealed. Its truth flies in the face of everything we value as humans. No religious performance can gain the favor of our Holy God; we must receive this gospel humbly as a gift from a gracious God. But when we read about the God of Genesis three, and the Lord Jesus of Philippians two, our hearts fill with wonder. Who is this God who far transcends not only our understanding, but our sensibilities as well? We stand in awe, and worship the One who will own the worship of the nations forever and ever!

STUDY GUIDE

1. How do you respond to the statement: When Christ returns, every purpose of our Father's heart will have been fulfilled? (Philippians 2:9–11, 3:20–4:1) From the text what is Paul's response to it? How is your response different? What are the implications of that reality in your day-to-day life?

2. Philippians 2:3 talks about looking at others as more important than ourselves. Using Philippians 1:1–2:11, why is it important to do that? Using Philippians 1:1–2:30, how do we do that? What needs to change in our hearts and daily routines in order to grow in "preferring one another"?

3. Find and contrast the difference between our grasping to be filled and allowing Christ to fill us from the text of Philippians—all chapters. What areas of your life are "too important" to trust Christ to fill? From the text of Philippians, what disadvantage does that create? How can you nurture yourself and others to allow Christ to fill each of you?

4. Do you see Jesus as the fulfillment of Daniel 7:13–14? How does this scripture relate to Philippians 2:9–11?

5. Where do you find evidence of God's humility in Philippians? How do you respond to the thought that our God glorifies Himself in His humility? Support your answer from the text of Philippians. What challenges and encouragements does this raise in you?

6. What do we learn about God as He promised redemption when there was no repentance or confession of sin on the part of Adam and Eve? Support your answer from the text of Genesis and Philippians. What questions does this raise in your mind?

7. Did you see yourself as an enemy of God before you believed the gospel? How do you respond to the text in Romans 5:6–11? How do you need to grow in your response to these truths? Support your answer from the text of Philippians.

8. How do you process the thought that the gospel could never be invented, it must be revealed? From the text of Philippians, explain how it is that no one would ever create the Christian religion?

9. Since all of the Christian life is about becoming like Jesus, in light of Philippians 2, take five minutes in prayer to ask God where you need to grow the most. Take heart and be of good courage. Why? Philippians 2:13! Only God knows where you must grow next and He will lead you in it. Don't blow this off. Find an accountability partner if you don't have one already and ask them to hold you to the responsibility to grow in the area God is prompting you to.

PRAYER

Take some time to express the awe and wonder in your heart that God would humble Himself, become the lowest form of man and die the lowest form of death. Tell the Lord that you cannot begin to understand how the Lord Jesus would leave the presence of His Father, the glories of eternity and the worship of the angels and embrace the cross. Ask God once again to teach you the humility of a servant, and to build into you the heart of His Son so that you look more and more like Jesus.

I entreat Euodia and I entreat Syntyche to agree in the Lord. Yes, I ask you also, true companion, help these women, who have labored side by side with me in the gospel together with Clement and the rest of my fellow workers, whose names are in the book of life.

Philippians 4:2–3

4

Agree with One Another

Toward the end of the first chapter in the Apostle Paul's letter to the church at Philippi, he called his brothers and sisters to let "their manner of life be worthy of the gospel." What does that look like? This call is lived out as we are seen "standing firm in one spirit, striving side by side for the faith of the gospel"! How does God bring us to that place?

Paul then describes the attitudes of the Lord Jesus that we must embrace if we would live in this "manner worthy of the gospel." As our Father builds into us the very heart of His own Son through the ministry of His Word and the power of His Spirit, we see how to live out this new Kingdom lifestyle in our church. Then God gives us the power of the indwelling Christ to make these relationships possible!

Later in his letter, just in case we are still confused about how to do this, the apostle gives us a real-life model to follow. Two women in the church at Philippi were struggling in their relationship with each other. Paul provides wise counsel for them, telling them how to navigate through this great difficulty:

> I entreat Euodia and I entreat Syntyche to agree in the Lord. Yes, I ask you also, true companion, help these women, who have labored side by side with me in the gospel together with Clement and the rest of my fellow workers, whose names are in the book of life. (Philippians 4:2–3)

What is happening in Paul's heart as he is reaching toward the conclusion of his letter? After writing about the strategic partnership they share, the glory of the gospel and our willingness to suffer for its sake, the power of the cross and the surpassing worthiness of Jesus, does he just now remember that he did want to make a comment on this situation between these two ladies before finishing his letter?

Absolutely not! Two issues prompted the writing of this letter by Paul to the Philippian church. One was his desire to thank them for the deep and full partnership they shared in the gospel, not only financially, but suffering with him, and confirming the gospel together before the eyes of the watching world. The other issue that prompted this letter was the division between Euodia and Syntyche.

SINS, HURTS, DISAGREEMENTS AND DISAPPOINTMENTS

We do not know what had happened between them. It does seem obvious that they were not arguing about whether Jesus is truly God, or whether He had in fact risen from the dead. This was a personal issue. Something had happened, perhaps a hurt or disappointment, a failure or sin of one against the other.

Paul sets the solution clearly before them. He calls them to agree with each other. He then asks co-workers to help them to that place. He had begun what we have designated "chapter four" with a second call to "stand firm." Nothing quite shakes us like divisions in intimate relationships!

> Therefore, my brothers, whom I love and long for, my joy and crown, stand firm thus in the Lord, my beloved. (Philippians 4:1)

Why is this personal issue so important to the Apostle Paul? We have already seen in this letter that Paul is "all about the gospel." He is discipling this wonderful church to orient all that they are, and all that they have, around the gospel of Jesus Christ. Anything that distracts us from the primacy of the ministry of reconciliation entrusted to us is an enemy of the gospel.

Surely, you have seen in your own family, or perhaps your church, how great a distraction problems in relationships become. Issues with each other seem to immediately consume all of the energy available to us. Every conversation, every prayer, every moment of time and every resource of strength must now be focused on solving this problem.

Whatever had happened between Euodia and Syntyche was not only affecting their relationship with each other, it was affecting the unity of the Church at Philippi. This issue was distracting them from the work of the gospel, and Paul tells them how they must get through this: they need to agree with each other.

WE CANNOT DO THIS

Why does Paul place this exhortation where he does in his letter? He has just portrayed so beautifully, with such eloquence and power, the humility of Jesus. The very Son of God did not grasp onto what was rightfully His; He came as a servant. He laid down His life. Jesus humbled Himself.

What would it take for Euodia and Syntyche to agree with each other? They would need to humble themselves. When Paul calls them to agree with each other, this does not come across to these sisters as a mystical exhortation, there is no confusion about how they must respond. Jesus had modeled before them vividly how to do this, and now He lives within His people to make this possible, and the normal response of His children.

But we know very well that we cannot do this. In our churches in the West, and even increasingly throughout the world, it is not possible for us to walk in what is most basically Christian. Why can't we do what the Apostle Paul is calling these two ladies to do—to agree with each other? There are two devastating reasons.

First of all, we highly value the independence of the system in which we live, and have learned to see the gospel through the eyes of our culture. Our independent spirit and the individualism we so highly value make it very difficult to submit to one another. Alongside of this reality is our commitment to what we have learned to see as our highest good: the need to be right. We pursue our "rightness" and defend the positions we hold at any cost.

How much will we sacrifice for the sake of maintaining our rightness? We will destroy our marriage, we will split our church, we will walk out of an intimate and treasured relationship, because being right is more valuable to us than anything else. In fact, there is nothing we will not give up for the sake of being right. It is our highest good.

GOD IS OTHER THAN WHAT WE ARE

The second reason we cannot do this is because we love justice more than mercy. We are not like our God, whose holiness defines both His person and His nature. What does it mean for God to be holy? Surely He is pure and without sin. Yes, God is completely separated from everything evil. But the first definition of holiness is "other."

God is "other" than what we are. In every way, His uniqueness and separation from everything that we are fills our eyes with wonder, just as it does the angels around His throne. Sometimes we celebrate this aspect of God's holiness when we sing together "there is none like you!"

This is the place where we see most clearly that "we are not like God": He values mercy over justice, but we value justice over mercy. That is why we would not have promised mercy to Adam and Eve in the garden when there was no repentance on their part, or confession of their sin, or any sense of responsibility for their actions. We would have reminded them about the consequences of their choices. We are not like God; He is other than all that we are, in every way.

This is why we cannot do what Paul calls Euodia and Syntyche to do. Our commitment to justice over mercy prevents us from humbling ourselves and agreeing with each other for the sake of the gospel. Being right is a higher good than the ministry of reconciliation, and at whatever cost, whether it is a broken marriage, a broken friendship or a broken church, we will hold out to defend our "right position."

You may well be struggling with much of what I am saying here. On one level, this is very confrontational concerning who we are and our culture as Christians. On another level, it might seem very confusing when we talk about the attributes of God like this.

When we list out the attributes of God, or the characteristics of His Person, we must know that He is forever, and at every moment, fully every one of those qualities. God does not diminish one attribute at the expense of another. He is always fully just, for example. In His justice, God's wrath must be satisfied toward all of His enemies. That is why the cross was so terrible. God's hate-filled wrath toward His enemies and His righteous justice were poured out on His own Son.

But God is also always fully mercy. He loves mercy! He gave His own Son so He could cover us with His mercy. Because we are "in Christ" (Ephesians 1:3–14), and because all of our God's affections are focused on His Son, He loves us too, and pours His mercy upon us.

STRONGHOLDS AND HOLINESS

God is always fully all that He is, but that does not mean that His attributes always remain in balance. In the garden, God pursued us when we were hiding, and then He gave His Son for His enemies. God did this because His mercy overwhelmed His justice toward those whom He had chosen in His Son from the foundation of the world!

The Apostle James describes the heart of our God in this way:

> For judgment is without mercy to one who has shown no mercy. Mercy triumphs over judgment. (James 2:13)

Unless we see the heart of God revealed in Genesis three and Philippians two, we will not be able to humble ourselves and to agree with each other for the sake of the gospel, as Paul is calling Euodia and Syntyche to do. In our modern church culture, we struggle with a Christianity that is largely a "mental religion." It is rooted in insights, principles and theological concepts rather than transformed hearts and relationships that overflow with the life of God.

75

As I have grieved over the level of anger, pain, bitterness and broken relationships among us, I have often thought: "We worship the gospel well, we study it well, we preach it well, but we really don't live it very well." We have given ourselves permission to believe all the right things and yet live together in a way that far more clearly reflects our culture than the Kingdom. This reality exposes the spiritual strongholds Paul talked to the Corinthians about in his second letter:

> For the weapons of our warfare are not of the flesh but have divine power to destroy strongholds. We destroy arguments and every lofty opinion raised against the knowledge of God, and take every thought captive to obey Christ, (2 Corinthians 10:4–5)

In light of the humility of your Lord, Paul says to Euodia and Syntyche, agree with each other for the sake of the ministry. Whatever this issue is, put it down, take every thought captive to obey Christ, and get on with the work of the gospel!

WE WERE ALL WRONG

This ministry, now called "Leadership Resources International" began in 1970 as a one-to-one discipleship work named "Personal Ministries." Karen and I had been in youth work and began developing Bible study materials that would help new believers grow in their walk with the Lord. Even then, our hope was that those we taught would in turn help other believers to grow as well.

In 1981, through close friends and co-workers, Américo and Kathy Saavedra, I was invited to minister to the staff of HCJB World Radio (now known as Reach Beyond) in Quito, Ecuador, a beautiful mission with whom we shared projects and staff over many years. That was my first trip overseas, and when I returned home, one of our staff members, Linda Alford, asked about the trip. I responded: "It was wonderful, but I do not believe I will ever go overseas again. God has called me to minister to the church in North America!"

I have often thought of that story in light of how well I am able to discern the will of God! Since then, by God's grace, this work has flourished around the world to His glory. It is good to be reminded that God's ability to use us does not depend on how well we understand His leading, but on how well we follow!

When I first visited Ecuador, God opened to me a very special friendship with the President of HCJB World Radio, Dr. Ron Cline. He saw that the nature of our ministry was not only biblical, but very encouraging. I had long desired to follow the exhortation of the Apostle Paul when he said: "through the encouragement of the scriptures we might have hope" (Romans 15:4).

Ron challenged me to make our ministry available to other missions, and we did. Very soon, God was opening many opportunities to encourage missions and pastors overseas. In fact, we were receiving many more invitations than we could handle.

About the same time, a businessman in the Chicago area, where we live, had become disappointed in the last several churches he had attended. He was very wealthy; in fact, he had just sold his latest business for several million dollars. He decided to use part of that money to begin a new church. This time, he was going to do it right!

He was looking for the perfect pastor for his perfect church, and was introduced to one of the leaders of our ministry. This beloved brother was a great preacher, a strong leader, a sports hero, a war hero, and very handsome. The business man and the core around him called my friend to be the pastor of their new church. Because of our relationship, my friend invited me, and others from our staff, to teach in the new church.

They liked our ministry. Soon the church began to grow; they were attracting other wealthy, sports-minded, beautiful and successful people to their church. When they saw the overseas opportunities God was opening to us, the elders came to us and said: "Why don't you come and join our church. You will be our mission outreach. We will fund your staff and all of your work overseas!"

Of course, Karen and I were deeply rooted in our own church, and greatly involved in the work there. Even the thought of leaving our church was very difficult for us. But this was a dream come true for many on our staff and board of directors. All of our staff function as missionaries and "raise their own support." That work is very difficult, humbling, and exhausting. To think that we would be freed from that relentless pressure was a great answer to prayer. And funds for overseas projects always seemed to be limited. The promise of these incredible resources seemed to be an answer to our prayers!

I was concerned. I was troubled by the relationship between money, power and control. I was even more concerned when one of the elders came to me and said: "We think you should limit your ministry to like-minded churches." That statement, of course, was very confusing to me. I began to think about what a like-minded church might be.

Then I began to think about what the Apostle Paul's ministry might look like if he had limited his ministry to "like-minded churches." Surely, he would not have gone to Galatia, where false teachers were introducing legalism into the gospel; He would not have gone to Colossae where they were mixing the gospel with Greek philosophies. He definitely would have stayed far away from Corinth, with the divisions around personalities in the church and the spiritual gifts out of order!

I tried to communicate my concerns to our board and staff, but many of them were so caught up in the dream of unlimited funds and opportunities that they could not hear me. I found that I could not communicate well. I finally got so worn down in the process, I said: "If this is what you need to do, go ahead. I cannot do it." And I quit.

This was all incredibly embarrassing. I had never seen myself as a quitter. I did not realize how exhausted I was physically, emotionally and spiritually. I also had many fleshly attitudes I was battling with in this process. I burned out; I gave up. I quit!

God did meet us at that place. It took many months for our hearts and our relationships to be healed. I will tell you that the best part of this story, as painful as it was to experience, is that all of us involved in that challenging situation are still serving together today!

What did we need to do to get through this? We needed to agree with each other. The truth is that none of us was right in this situation; we were all wrong. That is the way it is in the Body of Christ: we are all wrong! It is only a matter of degree.

What did it take for us to agree with each other? We needed to humble ourselves in one another's eyes and agree that the work of the gospel that God had entrusted to us was more important than anything any one of us desired, or felt was right. This was all very confusing to navigate through, but we did have the model of our great God who exalts Himself in His humility, and the power of His own Son within us!

HOW DOES THE WORLD KNOW?

During the last hours that Jesus spent with His disciples before He went to the cross, He summarized for them some of the most important things He had taught them. In the Apostle John's gospel, these teachings are referred to as "the upper room discourse." After washing their feet and calling them to serve one another, Jesus said:

> A new commandment I give to you, that you love one another: just as I have loved you, you also are to love one another. By this all people will know that you are my disciples, if you have love for one another. (John 13:34–35)

So it is not by the sermons we are preaching, the songs we are singing, the buildings we are building, our great evangelistic and social programs around the world, or even by how correct our theology is that the world knows that we come from Jesus. They know that we are His disciples by the way we love one another. Our relationships validate the message we are proclaiming!

In a very short time, as Christ was seeking His Father's glory above all and interceding for His disciples, He prayed:

> I do not ask for these only, but also for those who will believe in me through their word, that they may all be one, just as you, Father, are in me, and I in you, that they also may be in us, so that the world may believe that you have sent me. (John 17:20–21)

The world knows that we come from the Lord Jesus by the way we love one another. The world knows that Jesus has been sent by the Father because of the unity we share. This is the gospel! Jesus has come into this world as a gift from His Father, and we are His disciples. This message is proclaimed as powerfully in our relationships as in our words! Our love and unity enable the message to be seen and to be received.

We have an enemy who desires to steal away the power of this glorious gospel preached through our relationships of love, humility and serving. As Satan puffs up our pride and amplifies the pain of hurts, failures, disagreements, disappointments and sins that happen when people who are made out of dust are living in a fallen world, he will lie to us about each other's motives and slander one another in our minds. In that environment, he will convince us that love and unity are not the most valuable stewardship of our relationships. It is far more important to be right.

> The glory that you have given me I have given to them, that they may be one even as we are one, I in them and you in me, that they may become perfectly one, so that the world may know that you sent me and loved them even as you loved me. (John 17: 22–23)

GOD'S GLORY DIMINISHES US

Have you ever wondered how the glory of God makes us one? I surely have! I used to think that the glory of God was so big, so beautiful and so powerful that it drew us all together in one common purpose. In our awe of God, we would, together, give ourselves to the common purpose of His message of love for this world.

I do not believe that anymore. The way the glory of God makes us one is that it diminishes us. It makes our pride, our hurts and our rightness very small. It is very difficult to see how big and beautiful our God is when we are so big in our own eyes.

How can we walk with God in that most awesome purpose of time and history, the earth being filled with the knowledge of His glory as the waters cover the sea, if all we can see is ourselves, all we can feel is our hurts and disappointments, and all that moves us is our own pride? When our vision of His glory surpasses our focus on ourselves, we can be drawn together to proclaim His beauty and His loving grace.

You have heard me say more than once in this section of our study that "we cannot do this." The call of our culture, which so exalts individualism, and the pride of our flesh, which passionately moves us to exalt ourselves, makes it impossible on any human level to humble ourselves and agree with each other for the sake of the gospel. But there remains a great hope!

After Paul displayed for the church at Philippi the wonder of Christ's humility, he reminded them of God's great work within them through the power of His Holy Spirit:

> Therefore, my beloved, as you have always obeyed, so now, not only as in my presence but much more in my absence, work out your own salvation with fear and trembling, for it is God who works in you, both to will and to work for his good pleasure. (Philippians 2:12–13)

HUMILITY AND OPPORTUNITIES FOR THE GOSPEL

When we began our study, I mentioned that the proclamation of the gospel included all of the New Covenant. As Paul focused on that message in chapter three of his second Corinthian letter, he contrasted the ministry of condemnation that brings death, and the ministry of righteousness that brings life. The hope of this New Covenant is that our God makes us sufficient for all He calls us to do (2 Corinthians 3:4–6)!

This is the same message Paul is preaching in Philippians two! We are very small; we are not adequate to live out a lifestyle worthy of the gospel. We cannot look at one as more important than we are. We cannot humble ourselves before one another. We cannot agree with one another for the sake of the gospel rather than holding onto our rightness.

But there is great hope in the New Covenant! God is at work in us. He is giving us the desire as well as every resource we need to do what pleases Him. His power is perfected in our weakness.

Jesus humbled Himself and came to this earth as a servant, and He died the lowest death. He did this in obedience to His Father, the author of our salvation. Jesus also knew that the gospel was not possible if He was not willing to humble Himself in this way. Christ's humility created the opportunity for you and me to experience God's grace in the gospel.

The same is true for you and me. When we face hurts, disappointments and divisions in our relationships and our church, our humility can create an opportunity for the gospel. As we reflect the heart of our Lord in the way we walk together, those who are watching are able to see that we have been transformed by the very gospel we have preached. Our love and unity will draw them in to become worshipers with us of the exalted Christ!

STUDY GUIDE

1. Find the verses throughout the book of Philippians that explain living "in a manner worthy of the gospel." What are the inward choices? What are the outward actions? Where do you see these elements in your life? How do you need to grow in this area?

2. When you first read Paul's exhortation to Euodia and Syntyche to "agree with each other," do you see this as a realistic solution to their problem? Why doesn't Paul ask his "true companion" to research the issue to learn who is responsible, and then pursue confession, repentance and reconciliation? Support your answer from the text.

3. Using Philippians 3:15–4:9, explain the roles and actions Paul expects Euodia, Syntyche, the true companion and God to take in bringing about the reconciliation of these two women.

4. How simple is the answer to this issue between the two women? Why is it important to resolve this situation? Support your answer from the text.

5. How do Paul's instructions challenge our individualism and independent spirits particularly in a culture that worships these traits? How do these instructions challenge us in times of hurt and disappointment?

6. Find the verses that express how God's humility is seen through Jesus, through Paul? How is that expression different in Jesus than it is in Paul? Support your answer from the text. How does this change your understanding of mercy? From the text, how are we to grow in our ability to live merciful lives even when the wrong has caused us suffering? Why should we bother extending mercy in the midst of our suffering?

7. What do the grace and peace of God do in our lives? What stands in the way of us having the grace and peace of God? Support your answers from the text.

8. How great an impact do you think broken church and family relationships have on the gospel message? How does that fit with Paul's exhortation to agree and rejoice in the Lord?

9. How are we to combat Satan's attempts to amplify our pride and pain in times of hurt in your relationships through negative attitudes or thoughts about the person

with whom you are having difficulty? Support your answer from the text.

10. How can we fully embrace the hope and the power of the New Covenant, through which God gives us the desire and the power for all He calls us to do, even in times of personal hurt and disappointment? Support your answer from the text. Is it true that God has given us every resource we need in order to walk in the ways that bring Him the most glory?

PRAYER

Begin your prayer time by confessing that you are not like God. Admit to Him that you are most prone to value justice over mercy rather than embracing His love for mercy with justice. Ask God, once again, to give you the heart of His Son, and to make you like Jesus. Pray that God would give you a renewed vision of His glory, so that His eternal worthiness and humility would diminish your pride in times of hurts and disappointments with brothers and sisters and that He would reveal Himself to the world through your love and unity.

Indeed, I count everything as loss because of the surpassing worth of knowing Christ Jesus my Lord. For his sake I have suffered the loss of all things and count them as rubbish, in order that I may gain Christ.

Philippians 3:8

5

Our Passions and the Surpassing Worthiness of Jesus

As the Apostle Paul begins the third chapter of his letter, he once again calls this beloved church to rejoice. Given the realities of the financial poverty of the churches in Macedonia and Paul's imprisonment, we are reminded once again of the "inside out" nature of this joy. The source of Paul's joy, and that of his brothers and sisters, is the presence of God with them in their circumstances, and the confidence that He is working out His purposes through them and for them.

Paul's joy as he writes now is found in the truth of the gospel:

> Finally, my brothers, rejoice in the Lord. To write the same things to you is no trouble to me and is safe for you. (Philippians 3:1)

Everywhere Paul went, he was "dogged" by the party of the circumcision from Jerusalem! These false teachers claimed that to be a true Christian, a person not only had to believe in Jesus, but also needed to be circumcised and follow the law of Moses. Just as Jesus did with the Pharisees, Paul reserved his strongest language and expressed his greatest anger toward these prideful and manipulative enemies of the gospel.

> Look out for the dogs, look out for the evildoers, look out for those who mutilate the flesh. For we are the circumcision, who worship by the Spirit of God and glory in Christ Jesus and put no confidence in the flesh— (Philippians 3:2–3)

Religious people always tend to focus on the outward things that can be measured by spiritual performances. We can easily see, in these systems, how well we are following God by looking at how consistently we are observing the traditions that have been certified as proper by our leaders.

Jesus revealed this hypocrisy when He confronted the scribes and Pharisees about their focus on outward things while the inside remained filthy.

> Woe to you, scribes and Pharisees, hypocrites! For you clean the outside of the cup and the plate, but inside they are full of greed and self-indulgence. You blind Pharisee! First clean the inside of the cup and the plate, that the outside also may be clean. (Matthew 23:25–26)

Now, those same teachers were troubling the church at Philippi! In the eyes of many, it is always "safer and more measurable" to place our hopes and spiritual securities in the outward observances of the law, and physical signs such as circumcision, rather than a simple heart of faith.

Paul makes it very clear in his letter, defining the true gospel, that we are the genuine children of Abraham, and the true circumcision, when we reject any confidence in who we are and what we are able to do. We have placed every hope for now and eternity in who Christ is, and what He has done.

I CAN DO THIS

Somewhere around 1970, I went to our local hospital to visit my sister, Kathy. She had just given birth to her son Kenny, and I wanted to see her and meet my new nephew. After visiting with my sister for a bit and making sure she was well, I went to the window of the nursery where the newborns were lying in their bassinettes.

As I was trying to find Kenny, a man walked up alongside me. His wife had also just given birth, and he was there to see his newborn daughter. I turned to look at him and was struck by how handsome he was; truly one of the most beautiful human beings I have ever seen! We began to talk, and I was immediately caught up in his eloquence and his charisma.

This man would later change his name to Muhammad Ali. He had been stripped of his crown as heavyweight boxing champion because of his resistance to the Vietnam war, and I asked if he thought he would ever return to boxing. I had followed his career, and I was a real fan! After assuring me that he would fight again, we talked for several more minutes.

He learned that I was a Baptist minister, and then told me that he had just converted to Islam. I was intrigued. Why would he leave his Christian heritage for what seemed to me a foreign religion? "I can do this," he said!

We cannot "do" the gospel! There are no outward measurements by which we can secure our faith and gain approval by our God. In no other religion do we need to humble ourselves in order to become a member. This gospel is about hearts. It is all about the inside of the cup! Our glory and our worship are rooted in Christ and in His cross.

THIS IS JESUS'S GOSPEL

We must remind ourselves that this is not the gospel of the Apostle Paul. This is the gospel Jesus preached at the beginning of His ministry:

> Now after John was arrested, Jesus came into Galilee, proclaiming the gospel of God, and saying, "The time is fulfilled, and the kingdom of God is at hand; repent and believe in the gospel." (Mark 1:14–15)

This is the gospel preached by the Apostle John:

> But to all who did receive him, who believed in his name, he gave the right to become children of God, who were born, not of blood nor of the will of the flesh nor of the will of man, but of God. (John 1:12–13)

This is the gospel Jesus preached to Nicodemus:

> And as Moses lifted up the serpent in the wilderness, so must the Son of Man be lifted up, that whoever believes in him may have eternal life. For God so loved the world, that he gave his only Son, that whoever believes in him should not perish but have eternal life. (John 3:14–16)

This is the gospel preached by the Jerusalem council when God had brought salvation through faith to the gentiles. Even in those early days of the church, some were preaching the law and circumcision, but the elders and the apostles affirmed together the message of the gospel.

> Now, therefore, why are you putting God to the test by placing a yoke on the neck of the disciples that neither our fathers nor we have been able to bear? But we believe that we will be saved through the grace of the Lord Jesus, just as they will. (Acts 15:10–11)

WHAT A RÉSUMÉ!

Now, Paul does something very intriguing as he makes his case that the gospel is the only way to gain the approval and acceptance of our great and holy God:

> [T]hough I myself have reason for confidence in the flesh also. If anyone else thinks he has reason for confidence in the flesh, I have more: circumcised on the eighth day, of the people of Israel, of the tribe of Benjamin, a Hebrew of Hebrews; as to the law, a Pharisee; as to zeal, a persecutor of the church; as to righteousness under the law, blameless. (Philippians 3:4–6)

It is as if Paul is saying to those who place their confidence in measurable spiritual acts: "You think you have performed well? Let me tell you about my life before I met Christ!" Is there any Pharisee, any reader of this letter to the Philippians, any great preacher today who can measure up to Paul's life before his conversion? What an amazing man; what incredible accomplishments! Even when measured by the law, Paul was blameless.

Who of us would ever boast like that? But Paul does not want to put the glory of a life well lived on display; he is leading his readers, and you and me, to boast in Christ alone. He is making his point well: "If anyone could have gained God's approval through spiritual performances, it was me!"

When we read his words, we know that when Paul was still a young man, sincere in his heart before the Lord, he looked at the most valuable things to pursue, and the very best man he might become. He gave himself to the pursuit of those things with all of his heart, all of his life. As a result of those passionate pursuits, he became a model for all who would live a righteous, religious life

> But whatever gain I had, I counted as loss for the sake of Christ. Indeed, I count everything as loss because of the surpassing worth of knowing Christ Jesus my Lord. For his sake I have suffered the loss of all things and count them as rubbish, in order that I may gain Christ (Philippians 3:7–8)

Now, in the most vivid terms possible, Paul tells us what he did with all of those spiritually affirmed accomplishments that made the outside of his cup acceptable. Whatever he had gained, he rejected. Whatever was acceptable in the eyes of the men and women around him, he knew now earned him nothing before a holy God.

AN EXCHANGED LIFE

He calls these things "rubbish." All he had lived for with all of his heart, all of his life were not gain, they were loss. In fact, Paul uses the most graphic word he can think of to describe what he had seen as most valuable in his life. In some of our older translations, rubbish is translated as "dung." Yes, that is exactly what this great apostle is saying. Nothing more than a pile of manure!

> [A]nd be found in him, not having a righteousness of my own that comes from the law, but that which comes through faith in Christ, the righteousness from God that depends on faith— (Philippians 3:9)

Paul exchanged the righteousness that he had hoped to gain by keeping the law for the righteousness that God gave to him when he placed his faith in Christ. This is a wonderful description of the Christian experience. This is an exchanged life! We exchange whatever favor we had hoped to gain before God by doing the right religious things for what Jesus did for us through His shed blood on the cross. We exchange our death for His life, our depravity for His holiness, our emptiness for His fullness, our hopelessness for an eternity with Him! This is an exchanged life.

There is only one way to a right relationship with God: through faith in His Son. To be "found in Him" who is the center of our God's affections is the only way to salvation, and the only place of security and joy for our hearts.

> that I may know him and the power of his resurrection, and may share his sufferings, becoming like him in his death, that by any means possible I may attain the resurrection from the dead. (Philippians 3:10–11)

IGNITION POINT

We can sense the passions of Paul's soul rising as we read his letter. He is not only grateful that this God who had demanded nothing less than the perfection of holiness in order to be accepted by Him has now made a way through His Son, Paul is driving with all of his heart toward a relationship with Christ that is characterized by intimacy and power. Whatever it costs—imprisonment, suffering, enduring false teachers, even death; he is willing, at any expense, to know his Lord, and to look forward to the fullness of His presence in the resurrection.

How was Paul changed from a religious Pharisee who had dedicated himself to killing and enslaving Christians to a passionate and aggressive follower of Jesus? We find the record of his conversion in the book of Acts.

> But Saul, still breathing threats and murder against the disciples of the Lord, went to the high priest and asked him for letters to the synagogues at Damascus, so that if he found any belonging to the Way, men or women, he might bring them bound to Jerusalem. (Acts 9:1–2)

It was only a short time earlier that Saul of Tarsus was giving his approval to the stoning of Stephen. We can see how deeply the passions of his soul were engaged in defending the faith of his fathers. This new sect of believers in Jesus had to be destroyed in order for God's pure purposes to be fulfilled.

> Now as he went on his way, he approached Damascus, and suddenly a light from heaven shone around him. And falling to the ground, he heard a voice saying to him, "Saul, Saul, why are you persecuting me?" (Acts 9:3–4)

God did have purposes to be fulfilled among His people, and Saul of Tarsus was part of His means to those purposes! The life of this religious Jew was being invaded by the Lord Jesus Himself. Paul knew that this was nothing less than God speaking to him from heaven.

> And he said, "Who are you, Lord?" And he said, "I am Jesus, whom you are persecuting. But rise and enter the city, and you will be told what you are to do." (Acts 9:5–6)

Jesus revealed Himself to Paul that day on the road to Damascus. He also made clear to Paul that from now on He would own every moment of Paul's life, every ounce of his strength, every purpose of his heart, and every passion of his soul. That is why Paul begins his letters often by referring to himself as "a bondservant of Jesus."

HE IS WORTH MORE

What had happened to Paul on that Damascus road? He was converted. What took place in that conversion experience? Did he realize that he was wrong about Jesus all this time and understand that He actually was the Messiah and the fulfillment of all of the Old Testament prophesies? Yes, of course! Did he believe now that Christ had in fact been raised from the dead? Absolutely! Paul became a Christian that day when the light of Christ shined on him and claimed him as His own.

Something more happened. The passions of Paul's soul were ignited toward Jesus when he saw Him that day. How else can we explain the ministry schedule Paul kept, the endurance of his sufferings, the level of his devotion to the gospel and the cries of his heart for the presence of his Lord?

We talked earlier in our study about this reality: Paul was passionate about the gospel because he was passionate about Jesus. He gave himself to the cause of the gospel because it bore the name of the One he loved the most. How were the passions of Paul's soul ignited so that he gave himself so freely, aggressively, whole-heartedly to preaching the gospel? Paul's passions were lit aflame that day on the Damascus road when he saw the surpassing worthiness of Jesus, and those passions became the fuel that so fully empowered him in the work of the gospel.

Saul of Tarsus knew the Old Testament scriptures very well. Somehow, though, his eyes were blinded to the promised Messiah all over the pages of the text. But God had chosen Paul from the foundation of the world to be His servant, the one who would carry the message of the risen Christ to the ends of the earth. God opened his eyes that day on the Damascus road, and he saw Jesus!

Paul knew well the God who wrote letters on stone, but now he met the God who writes on human hearts. He knew the law that condemns, but now he met the God who brings righteousness. He knew how to perform the expected religious rituals, but now he experienced the power of God within him. He knew all about glory that fades away; now he saw a glory that remains. Paul knew about the death in our souls when we cannot achieve what God demands, but now he saw a God who brings life (2 Corinthians 3:1–11).

When Paul saw Christ that day, his heart was captivated by the surpassing worthiness of Jesus. He looked into the face of his Lord and he said: you are more beautiful than I had ever dreamed! You bring life to those who trust in you! You are worth more than anything I have ever known!

Paul had seen his religious observances as worthy of his life. His acceptance and approval as a Pharisee was worthy of his life. His devotion to his God that drove him to destroy His people was worthy of Paul's life. But now, Paul had seen the surpassing worthiness of Jesus, and he would never be the same again.

WHAT IS WORTHY OF YOUR LIFE?

Our passions drive us to the gospel. Like the Apostle Paul, we will never be passionate about the gospel until we are passionate about Jesus. Just as we studied earlier, no program or method will unlock the key to our effectiveness in sharing Christ with our family, our friends and co-workers, although we gratefully receive as much help with communication skills as possible. No manipulations of guilt or fear, or pressure, will move us to missions and evangelism. Only the love of Christ can compel us to lay down our lives for the gospel.

Like the Apostle Paul, the passions of our souls become the fuel for the gospel. How are those passions enflamed that move us to the ministry of reconciliation? Those passions are only ignited in the surpassing worthiness of Christ. Nothing less can get us there.

As I mentioned earlier, we struggle greatly in our churches as we seek to move our people to pray, give and go for the sake of the gospel. Why do we battle so in this area? There are many reasons, of course, but the greatest battle point is in this area of our soul's passions. The sad reality for many of our people is that they have not yet confronted anything worth more than what they are giving themselves to.

What is worthy of our lives? Is our career worthy of pouring our hearts into? Is our marriage worthy of everything we are? Our family? Our investments? How about our sports and hobbies? These are all worthy pursuits. They are good things, even proper and right. But until we see the surpassing worthiness of Jesus, we will continue to give all that we are, and all that we have, to where we are already spending our lives.

How can we move out of the malaise of continually giving ourselves to the good things of our past experiences? Ask God to show you in a new way, on a new level, the surpassing worthiness of His Son! Pray for a renewed vision of Christ's beauty, and the eternal value of serving Him without reservation, with every resource of your heart and life.

DO ONLY AS YOU PLEASE

How would you like to live for the rest of your life doing only as you please? If you could wake up each morning and say: "Today I am only going to do what gives me the most pleasure," wouldn't that be wonderful? That is exactly the place where God wants us to live every day, all of our days!

That is how the Lord Jesus lived each day. He found His deepest joy in bringing pleasure to His Father.

> So Jesus said to them, "When you have lifted up the Son of Man, then you will know that I am he, and that I do nothing on my own authority, but speak just as the Father taught me. And he who sent me is with me. He has not left me alone, for I always do the things that are pleasing to him." (John 8:28–29)

The satisfaction of bringing pleasure to his Lord moved Paul to serve with every resource every day, and to lay down his life for the name of Christ.

> Yes, we are of good courage, and we would rather be away from the body and at home with the Lord. So whether we are at home or away, we make it our aim to please him. (2 Corinthians 5:8–9)

Our ministry of TNT (Training National Trainers) has flourished throughout Asia. Not too long ago, in a country there where severe persecution remains a terrible reality, one of our TNTers, Amos, was arrested for preaching while he was training his second generation of pastors, following our commitment to equip national pastors to train other pastors in their own language and culture. He was brought into an interrogation room and was strung up over a beam by a rope tied to his thumb and his big toe. After suffering for many hours, he was beaten and thrown out into the street.

Amos continued his preaching and training. Some time later, he was arrested again. This time, as he was brought into the interrogation room, he saw another pastor strung up over the same beam by the rope attached to his thumb and big toe. The interrogator said to Amos: "Sit in this chair and watch him. I will return."

When the interrogator left, Amos quickly moved his chair under his fellow servant. Soon the interrogator returned and asked: "Who moved that chair"? Amos admitted that he had moved the chair in order to bring some relief to his hurting friend. Again, Amos was beaten and thrown into the street.

Amos continued to give himself to the gospel. Should we be grateful that another servant of our Lord was there to meet Amos when he was thrown into the street, and to remind him to endure in his suffering and to not give up on the gospel? No, there was no one there to meet Amos, and no one was needed! Amos is doing only what pleases him. He is serving the One who brings him the greatest pleasure he has ever known.

Like Pastor Tham, who we met earlier in our study, Pastor Amos would explain why he does this: "Because He is worth it"!

MEASURED AND POURED OUT

I am so glad that both the Apostle Paul and our friend Amos missed the seminar on "The Balanced Christian Life." What an enemy of the gospel! This is merely a human understanding of how to navigate complex responsibilities in a pressure-filled world.

All of us seem to have more responsibilities in our lives, relationships and ministries than we can possibly handle. Our lives are very full, and sometimes we become confused about where to give ourselves first in order to be good stewards of what God has entrusted to us. Some would counsel us that the answer in the face of pressure and confusion is to balance our responsibilities so that when every need is in its proper place, we can, in proportion, give ourselves to these responsibilities.

There are two very real difficulties with this perspective. First of all, none of us is smart enough to figure out how to properly balance the many roles and responsibilities that have been entrusted to us. We also lack the discipline needed to discern how to give ourselves properly, sufficiently, to our marriage, family, work, ministry, personal needs, sports and hobbies. This is why God has given us His Holy Spirit! He is able to show us how to give ourselves to the people and the work God has given to us as we seek His leading.

Secondly, the "balanced Christian life" is not a biblical concept. It sounds so right, and even helpful to us as we seek to live as good stewards of God's grace. The great problem is that this human philosophy leads to "measured out lives." We carefully measure our resources of time, strength, etc., in their proper proportion. But God has never called us to measure out our lives; He has called us to pour out our lives. This is Paul's testimony:

> Even if I am to be poured out as a drink offering upon the sacrificial offering of your faith, I am glad and rejoice with you all. Likewise you also should be glad and rejoice with me. (Philippians 2:17–18)

Measuring out our lives is anathema to the gospel! We are called to lay down our lives for Christ and His Kingdom.

When we live poured out lives, the questions that we ask are completely turned around. We begin to ask: "How much can I give away, and how much do I need to keep for myself? How much time can I give to encourage my brothers and sisters, and how much time do I need to spend on myself? How many of my prayers should properly be consumed on myself, and how many can I give to the gospel and the Kingdom?"

This new but simply normal Kingdom lifestyle happens only when the passions of our soul are enflamed toward Jesus. Those flames are only ignited when we see the surpassing worthiness of God's beautiful Son!

STUDY GUIDE

1. From the text of Philippians, why do religious people tend to focus on outward performances rather than the inward realities of the heart? What are the outward expectations you have of Christians? Discuss with each other the areas in your life that need change.

2. How would Paul respond to Mohammed Ali's statement: "I can do this"? Support your answer from the text. What does Paul say are the repercussions of doing it ourselves? As Christians we certainly acknowledge that our salvation isn't something we can do. However, what areas of life do you not pray over, thereby not letting the Lord in?

3. It is obvious that Paul excelled at "doing" Judaism, but then exchanged his achieved righteousness for the righteousness that comes through faith. Explain the difference Paul describes. Explain how you have experienced the exchanged life in Christ.

4. Why is it important to talk to Christ about our passions? Support your answer from the text. What areas of your life feel too dirty, mundane or trivial to talk to God about? According to Philippians, what does God want to do for you in those areas?

5. Using the text, define who Jesus is. In light of your passions, what is His worth? What keeps you from letting Him put every passion in perspective with Him? Why is it important to ask Him to do so? Support your answer from the text.

6. Paul describes several struggles that seek to pull attention away from missions, evangelism and prayer for the gospel in the world? What are they for Paul, for those he is in ministry with, those he is writing to? What distracts you and your church family? How does Paul instruct us to overcome these struggles?

7. In the progression of Paul's teaching in 2 Corinthians 5:14–21, where the apostle leads us to the ministry of reconciliation, which step is the weakest place in your life or in your church?

8. Biblically speaking, what does it mean to do only as you please every day for the rest of your life? Is it possible? How? Support your answer from the text. What priorities in your life need to change moving forward?

9. When we say "balanced life" what are we trying to reconcile? When Paul discusses it, Philippians 1:20–22, what is he trying to reconcile? How do you respond to the contrast between a balanced life and a poured out life? What changes do you need to make so that your life balance struggle becomes a life poured out?

10. Paul's aggressive walk in evangelism and missions was fueled by His love for Christ, and those passions were ignited in the surpassing worthiness of the Lord Jesus. What area of life are you walking aggressively in? What are the areas, scheduling, fitness, career, food, education, beauty, etc. that you pursue without including Christ in the process? Why not? What do you need to do for Paul's experience to become your own?

PRAYER

Begin your time of prayer by confessing how you trusted in your own goodness, or your religious performances, to be acceptable to God before you understood the hope of righteousness by faith. Ask God to give you the humility you need before Him to become His child, and to live out the Christian life. Pray that, like Paul, the passions of your soul would be ignited in the surpassing value, beauty and worthiness of Christ so that your life might be spent for His glory and His gospel on the earth.

That I may know him and the power of his resurrection, and may share his sufferings, becoming like him in his death, that by any means possible I may attain the resurrection from the dead.

Philippians 3:10–11

6

The Gospel and the Fellowship of His Sufferings

I have had the privilege of serving with one of my favorite organizations, Joni and Friends, for several years. Founded by Joni Earickson Tada, this is a wonderful ministry to individuals and their families who have been touched by this broken world, resulting in much physical and emotional pain. Joni was paralyzed in a diving accident at 17, and after much suffering physically, emotionally and spiritually, God filled her with His life and His joy, and gave her a vision to bring the healing love of the Lord Jesus, and His joy, to others with disabilities. Joni is one of the most beautiful servants of the Lord that I have known, and she and her staff bring the heart of our God to hurting people like no other work I have seen.

LIVING IN THE SHADOW OF THE CROSS

A few years ago, I was serving as the pastor at one of their Family Retreats. During those days, in addition to messages from the scriptures to both staff and families, I try to spend as much time personally with people as possible. One afternoon, I met with a young couple who were struggling with some hurt and confusion concerning their past.

This young wife had grown up on the mission field in Africa, and in order for her parents to fulfill the work to which God had called them, they sent her to a school designed for missionary children. This school was in another country in Africa, and she felt alone, very confused, and even abandoned by her parents. This pattern took place over the many years of her parent's ministry and her education. She loved her mom and dad. She wanted to help them, and to serve the Lord in that way, but the hurts and confusion remained.

As we sat and talked together, it became obvious that this young woman deeply loved the Lord, and loved her parents as well. In fact, when I asked her what her relationship with her parents was like today, she told me that it was great! They lived close to one another, spent time together often, and her mom and dad loved helping with their growing family.

But the sense of abandonment remained in this young woman's heart. How could her parents leave her alone like that? For many years, sending children far away to a mission school has been the pattern for many missionary families. But for her, the feelings of loss and aloneness affected her deeply. Was the ministry more important to her parents than their own daughter?

The more we talked, it became obvious that God had already accomplished a great work of healing in this young woman's heart, and His keeping grace was so evident in her, in her loving husband and in their family. We talked and prayed together, thanking God that her parents had done the best they could as they sought to follow God's call, and at the same time meet their family's needs. I then reminded her and her husband that we cannot take the Cross out of ministry. The shadow of the Cross moves over our lives again and again during the years that we walk with the Lord, loving and serving Him. This is one of the places the Cross had touched her life.

A CHURCH BORN AND CARRIED
THROUGH SUFFERINGS

When the Apostle Paul began his letter to the church in Philippi, he thanked them for their partnership with him in the gospel. A major aspect of that partnership was how they joined with Paul in his sufferings. He made that clear when he said:

It is right for me to feel this way about you all, because I hold you in my heart, for you are all partakers with me of grace, both in my imprisonment and in the defense and confirmation of the gospel. (Philippians 1:7)

How did the church at Philippi join with Paul in His sufferings? Surely, they supported him financially even though they themselves were struggling with poverty. They longed for his presence among them and the encouragement he brought to them. They prayed for his care, his protection and his deliverance.

We remember that the church at Philippi was born in the midst of suffering. Paul and Silas were singing hymns at midnight in that Philippian jail when the earthquake released the prisoners. The jailer who intended to kill himself was instead given life through the Christ he came to worship. He and his family were baptized, and this beloved church was born that night in a Macedonian dungeon.

The Philippian church was also cared for and shepherded in the midst of sufferings. Of course, Paul is suffering as he writes this letter from a Roman prison. Epaphroditus traveled between Paul and Philippi, bringing both news and encouragement. He would return to Paul with gifts from his brothers and sisters in Philippi that would help to sustain him in his imprisonment.

Epaphroditus was sick unto death when Paul wanted to send him to Philippi. Once again we see the depth of affection that filled these ministry relationships, but we also see that the gospel carried through the sufferings of God's people.

For he has been longing for you all and has been distressed because you heard that he was ill. Indeed he was ill, near to death. But God had mercy on him, and not only on him but on me also, lest I should have sorrow upon sorrow. (Philippians 2:26–27)

Paul's imprisonment, Epaphroditus' sickness, the poverty of the Philippian church, and sorrow all around. This is the environment in which the gospel was brought to Macedonia. This is the way too, that the gospel came to all of the new believers in Philippi who would place their faith in Christ and join this amazing fellowship of believers.

WHY THIS STRANGE DESIGN?

Paul's longing for his Lord included the desire to share in the fellowship of His sufferings. Like all of the apostles of Jesus, except the Apostle John, Paul would physically give his life for the gospel. When we follow Him, we, too, are called into the fellowship of His sufferings.

Why did our God design the gospel of His Son to be carried to the world through the sufferings of His people? On one level, of course, this makes no sense to us. It fits neither our perspectives nor our images of how God works. We have great difficulty understanding on ever deepening levels that His thoughts are not our thoughts, and our ways are not His ways (Isaiah 55:8–9).

The reality of this relationship between our sufferings and the spread of the gospel offends our sensibilities. Who would follow Christ knowing that it would cost their life? Why such expense for His children? We know that God does not desire anyone to go to hell. Is that not what He said through Peter when He expressed His passion for the salvation of souls? Peter had been teaching on the soon return of the Lord, and the realty that it has already been a long time since He made the promise to come back for us. And, of course, for us this promise is now two thousand years old!

> The Lord is not slow to fulfill his promise as some count slowness, but is patient toward you, not wishing that any should perish, but that all should reach repentance. (2 Peter 3:9)

The reason it has been so long between His promise to return and its fulfillment is not because our God is slow. He is patient. He does not anyone to perish. He wants everyone to repent. He is waiting, giving more time for our family, our friends, our neighbors and the nations to repent, and to come to Him.

We well know that when God talks about His desire that no one should perish, it does not reveal His ordained will, but the desires of His patient and beautiful heart. But if God does not want anyone to perish, why do we hear the call to suffer as we hear the gospel? Wouldn't it make more sense to get people into the Kingdom, just asking them to believe in the death and resurrection of Jesus, and then to disciple them into the call to suffer? In this case, the prosperity gospel makes a lot of sense. Who wouldn't believe in a God who lives for the happiness of His children? If this "gospel" was true, and the pragmatic goal of ministry was to get the most people to believe, then this is the gospel we should preach!

But as we well know, this is not the true gospel. We are confident that God will save all those whom He has chosen, through the work of His Spirit and our faithful preaching of His Word. That preaching will be truthful, full of integrity and compassion, and motivated by our deep love for people and for our Lord. And the truth is that this is a very expensive gospel.

THIS IS A PRECIOUS AND COSTLY GOSPEL

As we know, too, this is not Paul's gospel; this is the gospel of Jesus. As Jesus called people to follow Him, He made that call very clear:

> And calling the crowd to him with his disciples, he said to them, "If anyone would come after me, let him deny himself and take up his cross and follow me. For whoever would save his life will lose it, but whoever loses his life for my sake and the gospel's will save it." (Mark 8:34–35)

It is obvious that Jesus's ministry goal was not in the largest numbers of followers. He was seeking those given to Him by His Father, and those who would embrace His cross as disciples. He was calling those who were willing to lay down their lives for Him and His Kingdom.

A disciple of Jesus and Paul's "son in the faith," Timothy, struggled with this reality as he pastored the church in Ephesus. Timothy was a young man, his spiritual father was in prison, and he was facing one obstacle after another among the leaders in Ephesus. Paul's last letter, very close to his death at Nero's sword, was aimed at encouraging Timothy to endure in his sufferings and to not give up on the gospel.

Paul reminded Timothy of the faith that had been passed down to him by his mother and grandmother, and then said:

> For this reason I remind you to fan into flame the gift of God, which is in you through the laying on of my hands, for God gave us a spirit not of fear but of power and love and self-control. (2 Timothy 1:6–7)

Why does Paul tell Timothy to "fan into flame the gift of God"? Why does he talk of fear? He goes on to add shame to the very real battle in which this young pastor finds himself:

> Therefore do not be ashamed of the testimony about our Lord, nor of me his prisoner, but share in suffering for the gospel by the power of God, (2 Timothy 1:8)

We can understand some of Timothy's struggles. Surely, as a young man, he is overwhelmed with the battles with fleshly leadership, false teaching, and self-centered people. But there is more. How can he confidently preach this gospel? How can he call people to believe in and follow Jesus in the midst of these current realities?

The leader of the movement is in prison, and is being threatened with death. Why should they believe? Timothy is not experiencing great success in his ministry or obvious blessing on his life. Is this what will happen to them too if they follow Jesus? Timothy is ashamed of Paul's chains, and he is timid as he pursues his ministry. We can understand why.

But even knowing the depth of Timothy's battles in Ephesus, Paul shows us something of Timothy's character, commitment, and love for those who need the gospel. Our costly care for this gospel and the people who must hear it is not always rewarded by their conversion of those to whom we preach, but our motivation overflows from our love for Christ!

> I hope in the Lord Jesus to send Timothy to you soon, so that I too may be cheered by news of you. For I have no one like him, who will be genuinely concerned for your welfare. (Philippians 2:19–20)

This is a precious gospel, and it is given to the world at great cost. It cost God great humility to give the life of His Son for the lives of His enemies. It cost Jesus the glories of eternity as He humbled Himself to come into this broken and depraved world, and then lay down His life at the Cross. It will cost every disciple of Jesus their life as they follow Him and take up His Cross.

What a strange design for the expanse of the gospel around the world! The gospel that gives us life costs us our lives. God brings His life to others through us at the expense of our lives. This is a truth seen from the beginning of time, when God sought Adam and Eve, and you and me, when we were hiding in the darkness because of the guilt, fear and shame of our sin. He promised redemption that day, but at great cost to Himself. It is His way; He brings life at the great cost of His life, and carries it to the world at the cost of our lives.

GOD'S MYSTERIOUS AND GLORIOUS WAYS EXPANDED

We had talked earlier about how the preaching of the gospel involves the proclamation of the entire New Covenant. Paul teaches us the heart of that covenant, as we saw, in his second letter to the church at Corinth. This covenant of life and righteousness, of power and glory is ours in the death and resurrection of Christ.

God has placed in you and me the message of His grace in this great gospel! As Paul continued in his letter to Corinth, he reminded us of how God brings that gospel through us to the world. His teaching underlines what we have been looking at so far in this chapter.

> But we have this treasure in jars of clay, to show that the surpassing power belongs to God and not to us. (2 Corinthians 4:7)

If we owned a great treasure, what would we do with it? If we suddenly found that we had inherited several ounces of gold, or many precious jewels, how would we respond? Well, if we did not immediately sell them, we would try to find the most secure place to protect and keep them!

What has God done? He has taken the greatest treasure the world has ever known and placed it in the most fragile container the world has ever seen! God has placed the invaluable treasure of His own Son, and the gospel that bears His name, in you and in me, a common earthenware jar. There is nothing special about us. We are so weak and vulnerable, not known for our attractiveness or innovative abilities, or our great resources to carry out what has been assigned to us.

Why did God place something so far beyond measure in its eternal value within something so common and so vulnerable— so of this world? He makes His purpose clear: He desires to display His glory through us. God wants to be the only explanation for our lives and our ministries.

DEATH IN US, LIFE IN YOU

God's strange ways did not end with placing the treasure of His own Son's life within us, that common earthenware jar. He then begins to break the jar!

> We are afflicted in every way, but not crushed; perplexed, but not driven to despair; persecuted, but not forsaken; struck down, but not destroyed; (2 Corinthians 4:8–9)

Paul tells us that we are afflicted in every way possible in this world. We confront the pain and brokenness of this present age again and again. But we are not crushed in the process, because God is our keeper. So often we are greatly confused along the way, but we do not give up hope, because God is there with us.

Some of us can remember times when we were in the midst of various afflictions, whether it was pain in our marriage, brokenness in our family, financial pressures, sickness, fear or rejection. Often in these times, well meaning brothers and sisters might come to us and say: "What do you think God is trying to teach you through this?" Most often our only honest response is, "I have absolutely no idea, but I am going to hold onto God until I get through it!" We are perplexed, but not despairing.

> always carrying in the body the death of Jesus, so that the life of Jesus may also be manifested in our bodies. (2 Corinthians 4:10)

The mysterious purposes of our God, that He fulfills His ministry of reconciliation at the cost of His children's lives, are challenging for us to grasp, and even more difficult to experience. Paul makes it clear. We are carrying in us the death of Jesus so that His life may be seen. Our endurance becomes a significant part of God revealing Himself to this world.

> For we who live are always being given over to death for Jesus' sake, so that the life of Jesus also may be manifested in our mortal flesh. So death is at work in us, but life in you. (2 Corinthians 4:11–12)

God is continually bringing us into situations where we die so that He can pour His life through us to others. Paul is talking about himself and his ministry team, but he is describing our experience of walking with God as well. God is bringing His life to those around us at the cost of our lives. He is using the afflictions we face to squeeze His life out of us, and give it to those around us. That is the nature of ministry, and the way God has designed the gospel to progress through history, and around the world. We can enter into this process only as we join with Him in the fellowship of His sufferings.

A CLASH WITH OUR WORLD VIEW, AND OUR LIFE EXPECTATIONS

Do we sign on for this level of commitment and cost when we receive Jesus as our Savior and Lord? When we decide to follow Him as His disciple, are we ready to lay down our lives like this? No, we are not. This is a price far beyond our understanding, a promise beyond our ability to fulfill. We do not know when we say "yes" to Christ's call in our lives what He will do with us as we follow Him, but we do know that He will be with us all the way to the end. We live in the confidence that when we see His face, we will also hear the words, "Well done, good and faithful servant, enter into the joy of your Lord!" (Matthew 25:21).

I have not known great sufferings as I have served the Lord. I have hardly even been uncomfortable as I have traveled overseas. Only rarely have I felt threatened. My only real cost is being separated from my beloved wife, Karen, because I treasure every moment I can spend with her. Over the past several years, we have spent at least one third of our time apart because of travel. My heart aches when I am away from her, and, I must admit, I count the days on every trip until I can be with her again.

Sickness is another issue, however! For some years I have battled serious cancer and very time-consuming chemotherapy and other treatments. What a distraction! Twice, I have been near death with pulmonary emboli, i.e., blood clots in my lungs. Both times God healed me by His grace and power, and restored me to Karen, and allowed me to continue to serve Him.

I will never forget when I was first diagnosed with cancer, and many brothers and sisters who love me said to Karen: "Why Bill?" Karen, who is both tough minded and full of faith (and I love her for both) responded: "Why not Bill!" We are afflicted in every way. What happens to others in this world happens to us as well. This is the reality of life in a fallen world. It is the result that is different for us; we are not crushed, we do not give up, because our God is there with us, and His grace carries us every moment, in every life situation.

We greatly struggle with God's ways in ministry, pouring out His life at the cost of our lives, because we are taught every day, in every way, to make the most of our life in this world. God's call is confusing to us. We are confronted here with the mindset of our culture, and how deeply our life expectations have been shaped by the world in which we live. Our dreams, especially as westerners, are very different than the call of the gospel. In one kingdom we gain our lives; in another Kingdom we lose our lives.

Another place where the real life call of the scriptures confronts those of us in the West is how the Christian life is lived out and experienced. Christianity in our context can too often become only a religion of the mind, centered in insights, principles and theological concepts. This kind of Christianity might grow into a "make believe" experience of discipleship that takes place only in the realms of thoughts and speculations, rather than one lived out in relationships and real life circumstances.

For example, we might find ourselves in a Bible study, and questions about persecuted brothers and sisters around the world are raised. A brother or sister might say: "I wonder, if someone put a gun to my head and told me that he would kill me unless I deny Christ, could I really do that?" (What are the chances of that really happening?) Of course, this is the wrong question, one only asked in the realm of mental speculations rather than real life. The proper question is: "Can I live for Christ?" If we can live for Him, we can die for Him!

It is difficult for us to understand how deeply our dreams and expectations for the Christian life have been shaped by our culture, rather than the scriptures. Suffering and following Christ do not fit together well in a place where we have inherited the American dream, but it surely does in the rest of the world! In my work in Russia, every time we meet with pastors there, many of them can tell of fathers and grandfathers who suffered imprisonment or death. While training Persian pastors in a former Soviet republic, I had the privilege of attending a baptism service. A ministry partner standing next to me said, "They are drawing a line in the sand! Now every friend or family member knows that they are irretrievable and will reject them."

OUR GREAT ETERNAL HOPE IN THE MIDST OF SUFFERING

The Apostle Paul closes this teaching on God's mysterious way of pouring His life through us to others by reminding us not only of His keeping grace, but how this process will lead to glory beyond description.

> So we do not lose heart. Though our outer self is wasting away, our inner self is being renewed day by day. (2 Corinthians 4:16)

This is actually the second time in this chapter that Paul uses this phrase "we do not lose heart." I am so glad that God knows how vulnerable I am to losing heart, to giving up in life and ministry. I am grateful, too, that He makes it His priority to keep my heart! Why do we not lose heart? Because even though we are wearing down emotionally and physically, God keeps renewing us on the inside.

> For this light momentary affliction is preparing for us an eternal weight of glory beyond all comparison, as we look not to the things that are seen but to the things that are unseen. For the things that are seen are transient, but the things that are unseen are eternal. (2 Corinthians 4:17–18)

This momentary light affliction? Paul is talking about all of our life in this world! Is he trivializing the deep wounds of our lives and the great loss and grief we have borne in our earthly pilgrimage? No, he is putting our pain in perspective. In light of eternity, these experiences are momentary and small in comparison to the glory awaiting those who have walked by faith through the confusing times of their lives. There is glory yet ahead! The gospel is true, and the Word of God has been faithful. Suffering now, glory later.

It is interesting that Paul talks about "an eternal weight of glory." What God has prepared for us in eternity is not only beautiful beyond description, it is "weighty." We often talk about a responsibility as a "weight." Perhaps this hope points to a stewardship in eternity that God has been preparing in us, and for us, as we reign with Him forever! Could it be that there will not only be glory in heaven, but continuing ministry as well?

Why would we respond to Jesus's invitation to follow Him and join in the fellowship of His sufferings, knowing that this will cost us our lives? Only when, like the Apostle Paul and like pastors Tham, and Amos, we are captivated by the surpassing worthiness of Jesus and the passions of our soul enflamed toward Him, will we, too, be able to say: "He is worth it!"

Paul expressed his level of joy, even in the midst of being poured out for the sake of the gospel in this way:

Even if I am to be poured out as a drink offering upon the sacrificial offering of your faith, I am glad and rejoice with you all. Likewise you also should be glad and rejoice with me. (Philippians 2:17–18)

STUDY GUIDE

1. How do you know when you are suffering for the gospel and not simply because we live in a fallen world?
2. How has the Cross of Christ touched your life in costly ways? Using the text, what was Paul's response to being in jail, people preaching out of spite, etc.? How have you responded when the gospel costs you something?
3. Reading through Philippians 1:12–28, what was the result of Paul's response? What was the result of your own response to suffering?
4. Why did you choose to become a Christian? Why have you chosen to remain a Christian and trust Christ with your life in spite of the suffering life brings and the gospel requires?
5. What makes the suffering in this life worthwhile? Support your answer from the entire book of Philippians.
6. What inner and outward encouragement and support does Paul tell us God gives those who suffer for His name?
7. What activities and attitudes does Paul encourage us to pursue to remind us that God is worth every struggle, pain and inconvenience and walking with us in these sufferings?
8. Have you ever consciously suffered for the gospel? Share that experience with the group and explain what made it worthwhile.
9. Have you ever suffered from the fallen nature of this world and seen Christ redeem it for His glory because you prayed? What was it that you prayed? How did God answer that prayer? How did your response to suffering and your answered prayer advance the gospel?
10. In groups of two or three, share how suffering and suffering for the gospel are different. Share how your own priorities have been changed because of suffering. Share how God has made suffering for the gospel worth it in your life.

PRAYER

Father, how can I express my gratitude and my worship before you in light of how you gave your Son for me, and how the Lord Jesus gave His life for my redemption. Surely this is a precious gospel! Please receive my acceptable worship, the giving of my body as a living sacrifice to you. Lord, I pray that you would enable me to keep your costly love always in the forefront of my mind and heart so that I can walk with you as we together carry your gospel to the world. Knowing that you have promised to be with me always, and that you will keep my life even into eternity, is a hope beyond measure in light of the fellowship of your sufferings! Thank you for your giving to me; please teach me more about giving myself to you and to those around me for the sake of your name.

Brothers, I do not consider that I have made it my own. But one thing I do: forgetting what lies behind and straining forward to what lies ahead, I press on toward the goal for the prize of the upward call of God in Christ Jesus.

Philippians 3:13–14

7

Our Past and the Power of the Cross

A fter describing for us vividly how God captured his heart for the gospel through the surpassing worthiness of Jesus, the great Apostle teaches us how the God of holiness and glory set his heart free to serve Him without hindrance or reservation.

> Not that I have already obtained this or am already perfect, but I press on to make it my own, because Christ Jesus has made me his own. (Philippians 3:12)

EMBRACING THE CROSS

What is Paul referring to here? He had just talked of his passionate desire to know Christ. Paul hungered to live every moment in the resurrection power of His Lord, and he well knew that this meant that he must first embrace the cross in every aspect of his life.

We will remember that Paul began what we call "chapter three" of his letter by confronting the legalists, the party of the circumcision that told new believers that in order to really be saved, they would need to not only believe in Jesus, but to be circumcised and then follow the law of Moses. This is why Paul argued so strongly for the righteousness that God gives when we place our faith in Christ, rather than any righteousness we might gain through religious performances.

Paul embraced the Cross of Calvary as his place of hope before this holy God who had invaded his life. No good thing he had done could earn him any favor in the face of this God who demanded righteousness as the price of acceptance. Only what God had done in His Son, Christ Jesus, at the cross could satisfy both His wrath and His holiness. Faith in His work was Paul's only hope; any confidence in any good he had done were a "dead end," for Paul and for you and me.

Embracing the cross meant more than salvation for the apostle. Paul was also willing to own the suffering, rejection and shame that the cross had brought into his life. The party of the circumcision was popular because its message appealed to those whose main concern is the "outside of the cup." There can be terrible filth on the inside, but as long as we look good on the outside, everything is fine! Things of the heart are not as easily measured as religious performances.

For Paul, orienting every resource, attitude and passion around the cross was a costly choice. He suffered great persecutions because he embraced its message, and he laid down his life to carry the message of that gospel to the ends of the earth. He knew that the cross was not only the place where Christ died, it was the place where Paul died as well.

> I have been crucified with Christ. It is no longer I who live, but Christ who lives in me. And the life I now live in the flesh I live by faith in the Son of God, who loved me and gave himself for me. (Galatians 2:20)

Now, as Paul writes to his beloved brothers and sisters in Philippi, he tells them with great humility that he knows that he has not "arrived" yet at the place he desires to be in his walk with Christ, but he is "pressing on." Isn't this a place of great hope for you and me? This is the story of our lives as well. We have not arrived yet, but we are pressing on. We do that because our God is giving us the desire and the power to live as He calls us, just as God did with Paul!

FORGETTING WHAT LIES BEHIND

Even knowing that he has not reached a place of perfection in his life or ministry, Paul made a firm and conscious decision about how to move forward.

> Brothers, I do not consider that I have made it my own. But one thing I do: forgetting what lies behind and straining forward to what lies ahead, I press on toward the goal for the prize of the upward call of God in Christ Jesus. (Philippians 3:13–14)

How emotionally charged are these words that the great apostle is using. "I press on, one thing I do, straining toward the goal." We have talked considerably about how deeply Paul's passions have been ignited and engaged toward Christ and His gospel. So now, his walk in life and ministry are aggressively driven by the freedom that Christ has given him in this gospel.

There is an upward call. This pilgrimage that carries us from the kingdom of this world to the Kingdom of our God always moves us closer to Him, it becomes fuller every day, it elevates us, lifting us higher every moment. We become more like Him, and we desire Him more and more.

> Let those of us who are mature think this way, and if in anything you think otherwise, God will reveal that also to you. Only let us hold true to what we have attained. (Philippians 3:15–16)

I love to hear Paul's gracious heart in his letters. He knew well that those who made a spiritual living by measuring outward performances would not bring this level of encouragement and hope to brothers and sisters who were still struggling a bit in their walk with God. They would want to quickly respond with more guidelines, more things to do so that success could be attained. But Paul felt no need to convince them that he was theologically right on this issue. He knew that God would reveal that to them in His time.

YOU NEED TO FORGIVE YOURSELF?

Paul told his readers: "What is behind, I leave behind!" Wow! How can this possibly be true for him? What is he talking about here? What did Paul have to leave behind?

He had just given us his spiritual résumé, which was strong, successful and righteous even when measured by the law. What did he need to leave behind?

We know that there is more to the story. The filth inside the cup of this very religious Pharisee was ugly. The putrid pride of his self-righteous heart produced a terrible stench before our holy God. Paul was a murderer. He gave his approval to the stoning of Stephen, the first Christian martyr (Acts 7:54–60). Paul gave his life to destroy what is most precious to our God, the body of His Son (Acts 8:1–3). Paul, surely, had some things to "leave behind."

But is this really the answer? It seems that in this Philippian letter, this is the second time Paul gives us an embarrassingly simplistic answer to a very large life issue. The first time was when we looked at the difficulty between Euodia and Syntyche. When the issue between them was threatening not only their relationship, but the unity of the church at Philippi, Paul's solution was for them to "agree with each other."

When we read Paul's counsel, we want to respond: "Sure, Paul, that will take care of the problem!" In our own hearts, we know how impossible it will be in the flesh for these two dear ladies to agree with each other! For Paul, the issue was very simple. The disagreement between Euodia and Syntyche was distracting them, and the church at Philippi, from giving themselves wholeheartedly to the gospel, so follow the model of the Lord Jesus who lives in you and empowers you, humble yourselves and agree with each other.

Now, once again, we seem to have received a very simplistic answer to a very large life situation. Many of God's servants want to give themselves to the work of the gospel, and yet they battle deeply with a sense of unworthiness and inadequacy. All of us have experienced terrible brokenness in our past. When our church gathers for worship on Sunday morning, the reality is that some of us who have come to exalt the Lord have sexual sin in our past. Some of us have experienced the deep pain of broken relationships. Some of us have fallen on our faces in places where we thought we never would again. Many of us have made choices that have devastated not only our lives, but the lives of others.

How do we get past the broken places, the guilt, the shame, and the unworthiness so we can still walk freely with God and serve Him with a whole heart? The Apostle Paul is teaching us right here, right now! "Forgetting what lies behind and striving forward" is the way God has made for us through the cross of His Son.

One afternoon, as I was returning from a meeting at my office. I had my radio tuned to one of our favorite Christian programs. The host was interviewing a very popular preacher who had written a very successful book on forgiveness. Now, he had written a follow-up book, and was back on the program with an interview to promote his new book.

The host asked him why he had written a second book on forgiveness when the first had been received so well. He responded: "Because we only dealt with half of the problem in the first book. In order to be really free, you need to forgive yourself."

Of course, I do not know the entire Bible, but my mind began to scroll over the scriptures that I know, trying to find a scripture that hints in any way that for us to live freely as God's children, we need to forgive ourselves. There is no text. This is human understanding layered over the Word of God. This is nothing less than a great war that has been fought for millennia by the enemy of our souls on the battlefield of our minds. He wants us to place our hope and confidence in what we do, rather than what God has done. Satan lives to convince us that we are not truly free because there is still more for us to do, new insights to discover, new steps to take, new principles to learn.

GOD'S GIFT: A CLEANSED CONSCIENCE

When Paul said: "Forgetting what lies behind, I strive forward," he is telling us how he sees the cross. He is reminding us that what God has told us about our sin is fully true in every way.

123

Paul had embraced the cross as the turning point of his life, and this cross became the place where God set him free from the depravity, failure and brokenness of his past so he could give himself without limitation to the gospel of Christ.

The writer to the Hebrews reviewed for the Jewish believers the work of God, in Christ, in the cross. Just as the Apostle Paul battled with those who wanted to preach another gospel, that we also need to be circumcised and follow the Law of Moses, the writer to the Hebrews continually confronted those who would preach any other gospel than that of God's grace in His Son.

> But when Christ appeared as a high priest of the good things that have come, then through the greater and more perfect tent (not made with hands, that is, not of this creation) he entered once for all into the holy places, not by means of the blood of goats and calves but by means of his own blood, thus securing an eternal redemption. (Hebrews 9:11–12)

The writer is contrasting for us the sacrifices of the Old Covenant, that is the blood of animals, with the sacrifice of the New Covenant, the blood of Christ. We will remember that when Jesus died on the cross, the veil of the temple was torn in two (Mark 15:37–39) from the top to the bottom. The writer to the Hebrews explains why. At the cross, Jesus entered an eternal place, not of this creation, but into the very Holy Place of His Father, and made atonement for our sins.

> For if the blood of goats and bulls, and the sprinkling of defiled persons with the ashes of a heifer, sanctify for the purification of the flesh, how much more will the blood of Christ, who through the eternal Spirit offered himself without blemish to God, purify our conscience from dead works to serve the living God. (Hebrews 9:13–14)

What a contrast between the sacrifices of the old and new covenants. The blood and ashes of animals are sufficient for cleansing the flesh, but the blood of Christ cleanses our conscience!

The rituals of sacrifice offered day after day throughout the centuries were all pointing to Christ and His cross. Not only pointing forward, but higher in hope and fuller in scope, from the temporary to the eternal, and from the outside to the inside. From the beginning, God was aiming at the filth on the inside of the cup, and the hope of internal freedom.

The sacrifices of the Old Covenant were like taking a shower. We can take a hot, soapy shower and feel very clean, but depending on what we do afterward, we know it might be a good idea to take another shower. It only washed off the outside, and was a very temporary cleansing! The sacrifice of Christ at the cross is different in every way: it is both internal, and eternal. His blood cleanses our conscience, and it lasts forever.

As we read the last words of verse 14, we know that the writer is talking about the center of God's purposes for our lives: He has raised us up to be His servants. But God knows that we cannot serve Him with all of the dead things from our past hanging on us. So one of the most wonderful gifts God gives to every one of His children is the gift of a cleansed conscience!

Our God knows that in order to live freely, confidently as His servant, we need to not only be completely free and clean in His eyes, we need to be completely free and clean in our eyes as well. So, He gives us this most beautiful and powerful gift at the cross; He cleanses our conscience.

THE ULTIMATE FOOTBALL GAME?

As the writer returns to this theme in his next chapter, he talks of the hope of God's people in the sacrifice of the Old Covenant.

> For since the law has but a shadow of the good things to come instead of the true form of these realities, it can never, by the same sacrifices that are continually offered every year, make perfect those who draw near. Otherwise, would they not have ceased to be offered, since the worshipers, having once been cleansed, would no longer have any consciousness of sins? (Hebrews 10:1–2)

When we read in the books of Leviticus and Deuteronomy about the requirements of the sacrificial system that the law demanded, we become exhausted just trying to keep up with it all even on a mental level. How could the believers in the Old Covenant possibly keep up with all that needed to be done to maintain a right relationship with God?

There was one great hope! One time each year, the High Priest could go into the Holy of Holies to make atonement for his sins and the sins of the people. They would look forward to that Day of Atonement with such hope: at last we can know the forgiveness of our God, at last our sins can be dealt with in the face of His holiness, at last we can be right with God again!

But the effect was just the opposite. Every year when the High Priest entered the Holy of Holies to make atonement for sin, rather than providing forgiveness and freedom in the hearts of God's people, it actually became a reminder of their sins every year. The continual, overwhelming, impossible sacrificial system resulted in a "consciousness of sins" within their hearts. This is the issue our God is confronting with the hope and freedom promised in the New Covenant!

> But in these sacrifices there is a reminder of sins every year. For it is impossible for the blood of bulls and goats to take away sins. (Hebrews 10:3–4)

Why is there a "reminder of sins year by year" resulting in a "consciousness of sins" in the hearts of God's people? Because it is impossible for the blood of animals to take away sins! The entire sacrificial system, whose requirements we could not possibly meet, was pointing forward to Christ. The Old Covenant was all about shadows of good things to come; the substance of all hopes for forgiveness and freedom are found in God's sacrifice of His Son, Jesus. He is able to make perfect all who draw near to Him.

There is a story told of a "press conference" a few years ago the week before the Super Bowl in the United States. No sporting event in our culture is as "hyped" as the Super Bowl! In fact, the day it is played each year has become like a national holiday.

At this particular conference, one of the event leaders was waxing eloquent at the podium about how this was the ultimate football game. All of the teams were represented at the beginning of the season, and then came the playoffs, and now only these two teams were left to battle each other for the trophy. This is the ultimate football game!

One of the football players happened to be in the audience. He raised his hand and said: "Excuse me, sir, but if this is the ultimate football game, how come they will play it again next year?"

I think that was exactly how God's people under the Old Covenant looked at the Day of Atonement. If this is the most we can do in order to be right with God, how come we will do it again next year? We do not have to do it again next year! God has provided one sacrifice for all of time and eternity, providing eternal redemption and internal freedom.

This is why Paul is free to leave his past behind, embrace the cross and press forward with his whole heart in the work of the gospel. All of his hope is in the finished work of our God in the cross of His Son.

NO REGRETS

In the cross, God dealt with not only the sin that separated us from Him, He dealt forever with the "consciousness of sins" that enslaved us to our past and stole away our freedom to serve Him. The Apostle Paul taught the church at Corinth about the power of that transaction in setting our hearts free for the gospel.

> As it is, I rejoice, not because you were grieved, but because you were grieved into repenting. For you felt a godly grief, so that you suffered no loss through us. (2 Corinthians 7:9)

Paul had written this church a very confrontational first letter, and he knew that his message had brought deep grief to his brothers and sisters. That grief brought sorrow to Paul's heart as well, because of his love for them. But now Paul expresses great joy because that grief led them to repentance. The genuine fruit of godly sorrow is true repentance.

> For godly grief produces a repentance that leads to salvation without regret, whereas worldly grief produces death. (2 Corinthians 7:10)

"Worldly grief," or the sorrow we know so well in our culture, produces death. The relentless regrets over our failures and depraved choices results only in an overwhelming sense of guilt and shame that imprisons us to our past. True repentance leads to salvation without regret.

Paul is surely referring here to the reality of our salvation experience. We never regret moving away from our sin and toward the gospel in response to God's mercy toward us. But there is a fuller reality for us here: the gospel is so powerful, it even deals with our regrets from the past.

Have you ever thought that the gospel is too good to be true? You are absolutely right; but it is true in every way! Only in Christ can we take all that we were, every place we have ever been, all that we have ever done, bring them to the cross of Calvary, put them down and walk away completely free, completely clean, with no regrets.

It is in the regrets that Satan gets his hooks into our hearts. How many of God's people, sincere in their desire to serve Him live in the regrets of the past? If only I had not fallen on my face back there. If only I had not chosen to do that, if only I had not become involved in that relationship. We want to follow Paul and "strain toward what lies ahead," but we have not "forgotten what lies behind." Only when we embrace the cross can we experience the freedom it brings.

IT IS FINISHED

In the treasure of Paul's letter to the church at Rome, he wrote to them the greatest headline the world has ever seen:

> There is therefore now no condemnation for those who are in Christ Jesus. For the law of the Spirit of life has set you free in Christ Jesus from the law of sin and death. (Romans 8:1–2)

Never, in all of time, in all of eternity, is there any condemnation awaiting those who have placed their faith in Christ! We live in the spirit of life, set free from the fear of sin and death that had so controlled the hearts of all who followed God in the Old Covenant. Why are such hope, confidence and freedom ours now because we are in Christ?

> For God has done what the law, weakened by the flesh, could not do. By sending his own Son in the likeness of sinful flesh and for sin, he condemned sin in the flesh, in order that the righteous requirement of the law might be fulfilled in us, who walk not according to the flesh but according to the Spirit. (Romans 8:3–4)

What the law could not do, God has done! What an amazing description of the power of the law. For millennia, the law had cried out "Do!" The demands were relentless, endless, impossible to fulfill. No matter how sincere the believer, there was always more to "do." Now, the cry of the cross has changed everything. God has said: "Done!"

> When Jesus had received the sour wine, he said, "It is finished," and he bowed his head and gave up his spirit. (John 19:30)

When Jesus had fully satisfied the wrath of the Father toward His enemies and made atonement for our sins, He released His spirit, and He died. There is nothing left for us to do now but to embrace His cross, forget what lies behind, strain forward to what lies ahead, and, like Paul, give ourselves to the ministry of the gospel!

STUDY GUIDE

1. When we forget that spiritual maturity is a thing of the heart and not what the "outside of the cup" looks like, who in Philippians are we like? What are the dangers of being like these two types of people Paul discusses? What needs to happen for us to know and/or remember where true spiritual maturity comes from?

2. Do you live consciously aware of sharing in Christ's death and resurrection? If not, how do you know you are sharing in it? Support your answer from the text.

3. How does Paul describe "embracing the cross"? What is so important about it? How does this compare with the "health and wealth gospel"? If God loves us then what is wrong with the "health and wealth gospel"? What do we miss out on when we choose what we want or think is best instead of pouring ourselves out to embrace the cross?

4. What does Paul mean by "forget what lies behind"? What is the difference between "straining forward to what lies ahead" and doing it yourself? Define maturity using the text.

5. Our enemy wants to convince us that we don't need to embrace the cross, but that we do need to do just one more thing. What things has he convinced you to do to get rid of your past or preserve your future? Why is it so difficult to believe that God will supply our needs, give us the strength to pour ourselves out, and satisfy our spirits with His grace and peace? In what ways do you desire more than what God offers? In what ways has what He offers proven to be more than you thought it would be?

6. Take a few moments and think through the negative things in your past that have been difficult for you to "leave behind." List them privately. What about these experiences makes you think that the blood of Christ shed on the Cross isn't enough? Is there healing that needs to happen too? Why is it difficult to believe that the cross can abundantly walk you through the healing process to leave you free? Pray over each other either in twos or as a group.

7. Take a few moments and think through the positive things in your past that have been difficult for you to "leave behind." List the things you're proud of and even currently want to be known for; do these things interfere with your

ability or willingness to embrace the cross? Pray that you would come to see Christ as worth any sacrifice as we were to Him.

8. Is it easier to "leave behind" our past or someone else's? Leaving behind the transgressions of others is a massive tangled subject that ranges from the petty nuances that have merely pricked our pride to the holding of our pride—that "at least we haven't..."—to the deep wounds of abuse. In the case of this discussion let's focus on the things that cause grudges or keep us from socializing with a certain type of person. What types of things keep you from welcoming certain people into fellowship with you? Is this a matter of enforcing a form of outward performance on others instead of accepting the inward work God is working to completion?

9. We know that to be justified before God means that in His eyes it is "just as if we had never sinned." How does this apply to letting go of the past? If it's as if we never sinned, why must we strive toward what lies ahead?

10. Satan uses regrets to get his hooks into us. Where does he do this to you and steal your freedom and confidence away? What does Paul give us to respond with? Philippians 1:27–30, 2:12–18, 3:12–4:7

11. What is the difference in practice between pouring out your life to the glory of God through the power of Christ Jesus and trying to "do" the gospel work you see a need for? Make a list of steps as a group. Compare the list to the text of Philippians.

PRAYER

Perhaps a good place to begin your group or your personal prayer is telling God that your heart and your mind are far too small to grasp these truths of the scriptures that we have studied here. The gospel seems far too good to be true! We will never fully understand God who gave Himself for us in order to make us free and clean in His love at the cross and then empower us to serve Him in the ministry of reconciliation. But we can worship Him and ask Him to enable us to love Him even more. Thank God for the cross, and take some group or personal time to worship Him now!

And the peace of God, which surpasses all understanding, will guard your hearts and your minds in Christ Jesus.

Philippians 4:7

8

His Presence; Our Peace

The Apostle Paul is discipling the church at Philippi to orient all that they are, and all that they have, around the gospel of the Lord Jesus Christ. He has been vulnerable toward them as he has shared intimately how God captured his own heart for the ministry of reconciliation. He was, in fact, an enemy of God, consumed with his own self-righteousness, until every passion of his soul became enflamed toward the gospel when he saw the surpassing worthiness of Christ.

Paul continues to give himself as a model for the Philippian believers. He had, in great humility, just shared with them that he had not "become perfect" in his walk with the Lord, but continued to "strain forward," and now with great confidence, he calls them to imitate what they have seen in him:

> Brothers, join in imitating me, and keep your eyes on those who walk according to the example you have in us. (Philippians 3:17)

What is necessary if we would become a model for young believers? Do we need to be able to point to a perfect record in our walk with God, or our service in ministry? Paul did not feel that perfection was a prerequisite to modeling. He had humbly talked about his own weaknesses and failures, and yet he calls his readers to imitate him. He wanted them to share his love for the Lord Jesus, his passion for the gospel, and his humility in serving.

> For many, of whom I have often told you and now tell you even with tears, walk as enemies of the cross of Christ. Their end is destruction, their god is their belly, and they glory in their shame, with minds set on earthly things. (Philippians 3:18–19)

It is fascinating how Paul describes the enemies of the gospel. He does talk about false teachers, or even those whose theology is suspect. Enemies of the cross are seen in their consumer mentality. They are not givers and servants; they are takers! They shamelessly consume resources and relationships in order to build up themselves. Their fleshly passions are the end of every pursuit, and they themselves are consumed in the end.

THE BLESSED HOPE AND OUR FREEDOM IN THE GOSPEL

In this world of users, takers and consumers, our God is raising up a new people. Rather than empty persons continually draining life from those around them, those in His new creation draw their life from Christ and lay down their lives in order to build up one another. Only out of our fullness, confidence and hope through Christ can we serve as life-givers in this new creation.

> But our citizenship is in heaven, and from it we await a Savior, the Lord Jesus Christ, who will transform our lowly body to be like his glorious body, by the power that enables him even to subject all things to himself. (Philippians 3:20–21)

Paul had been very open with his brothers and sisters in Philippi earlier in his letter concerning how he saw his future. His own desire was to leave this world to be with Christ. He was willing to remain here for their sake, but he longed for the presence of his beloved Lord. He was confident, however, that in God's time, He would fulfill the desires of Paul's heart. Paul would lay down the earthly tent of this body and receive from God in the resurrection a new body, fit for eternity.

Heaven is real, and our hope for eternity is in the resurrection. We will live forever in God's presence in a body just like that of the Lord Jesus after His resurrection. Paul had told his readers the truth about this dark world; suffering is part of the gospel. When we embrace the cross of Christ, we embrace not only the forgiveness, life and hope it brings, but we also embrace the shame and reproach, the cost to our own lives. But there is great glory in the gospel as well! We will fully know that glory in the presence of our Lord, when we share in His resurrection.

The Apostle Paul wrote to Titus about this blessed hope in this way:

> For the grace of God has appeared, bringing salvation for all people, training us to renounce ungodliness and worldly passions, and to live self-controlled, upright, and godly lives in the present age, (Titus 2:11–12)

In a way very similar to Paul's message to the church at Philippi, he taught Titus about how God's grace transforms us from takers and consumers to servants and givers.

> waiting for our blessed hope, the appearing of the glory of our great God and Savior Jesus Christ, who gave himself for us to redeem us from all lawlessness and to purify for himself a people for his own possession who are zealous for good works. (Titus 2:13–14)

We will never be free to give ourselves to the gospel while we are in this pain-filled world, and experience the sufferings we bear in this present age, unless we own the hope of eternal life, the power of the resurrection and the confidence of heaven. Paul lived every moment with his eyes on eternity, and he calls the Philippians, and you and me, to follow his example.

STAND FIRM AND REJOICE!

Now, Paul once again exhorts his readers to stand firm in the Lord:

> Therefore, my brothers, whom I love and long for, my joy and crown, stand firm thus in the Lord, my beloved. (Philippians 4:1)

We are reminded once again of the relationship Paul shared with this wonderful church. This was not only a group of new believers that the apostle was training in life and ministry. There was love, intimacy, longing, joy and genuine pride in their life together. When relationships like these are shared, there is also a place of power from which a teacher can move fellow followers in their walk with the Lord.

How do God's people stand firm in the Lord?

> I entreat Euodia and I entreat Syntyche to agree in the Lord. Yes, I ask you also, true companion, help these women, who have labored side by side with me in the gospel together with Clement and the rest of my fellow workers, whose names are in the book of life. (Philippians 4:2–3)

This is one more reminder that our relationships with one another become a mirror of our relationship with God. Our heart before the Lord is reflected in our responses to each other in Christ. Standing firm in God depends on whether we are willing to bring His heart to one another. Our ability to humble ourselves before one another, of course, reflects the attitudes of the Lord Jesus like no other response in the Christian life. Only knowing His heart on this level enables us to place the gospel as a priority over our own pride.

> Rejoice in the Lord always; again I will say, rejoice. (Philippians 4:4)

Living in the joy of the Lord helps us to stand firm as we give ourselves to the gospel. It is significant that Paul presents this as a command: rejoice! We might be tempted to think that since this is the great apostle writing, living with an attitude of joy might be easier for him than it is for us in the day-to-day battles of life. Then we remember that he is sending this exhortation from prison, probably chained between two imperial guards, and awaiting Nero's sword.

HIS PRESENCE CHANGES EVERYTHING

Earlier, we talked about joy that is "inside out." The joy that Paul is calling the church at Philippi to experience is not based on outward circumstances; it is the overflow of our confidence in God's presence and His power as He works on our behalf. Paul makes that clear as he continues:

> Let your reasonableness be known to everyone. The Lord is at hand; (Philippians 4:5)

What is the hope that undergirds Paul's encouragement? Is he saying: "Don't give up! It will be a very short time, and Jesus will return. Hold on!" That is possible, but in fact, Paul is setting before us one of the most wonderful truths of the scriptures. He is teaching us about the confidence, freedom and hope that flow in our hearts when God is there.

From the beginning of the scriptures to the very end, we find this amazing assumption on the part of our great Lord God: His presence changes everything! We will remember when God called both Moses and Joshua, He promised: "I will be with you." All of the sufficiency that flows from His presence would be theirs as they served Him. This is, of course, just as true for you and me.

From the beginning, God has desired to be present with His people. In the garden he walked and talked with Adam and Eve. He led His people through the sea by the pillar of fire.God was with them in the cloud as He led them through the wilderness. He made His home with them in the tabernacle. All of this was pointing to the gift of His Son:

> "Behold, the virgin shall conceive and bear a son, and they shall call his name Immanuel" (which means, God with us). (Matthew 1:23)

When Matthew quoted the prophet Isaiah, we see once again the desire of our Father to be present with His people. He would fulfill the hope of the prophets in the Messiah, the Lord Jesus. God would be present with us in Christ. Jesus, then, promised His Spirit after He returned to His Father.

And I will ask the Father, and he will give you another Helper, to be with you forever, even the Spirit of truth, whom the world cannot receive, because it neither sees him nor knows him. You know him, for he dwells with you and will be in you. (John 14:16–17)

John had begun this chapter by telling His disciples that He was going to make a place for them, and would return to take them to Himself, and to the eternal home He had prepared for them. Later in the chapter, however, as He answered a question from one of His followers, He told them something just as wonderful.

Jesus answered him, "If anyone loves me, he will keep my word, and my Father will love him, and we will come to him and make our home with him." (John 14:23)

In the meantime, before Jesus returns, He and our Father will come and live with us. Surely His presence changes everything! When we rejoice in Christ, emulate His humility and stand firm in Him we become more aware of God's presence and His indwelling Spirit of Holiness.

do not be anxious about anything, but in everything by prayer and supplication with thanksgiving let your requests be made known to God. And the peace of God, which surpasses all understanding, will guard your hearts and your minds in Christ Jesus. (Philippians 4:6–7)

Paul is giving his brothers and sisters in Philippi a wonderful process in which they can endure through the sufferings of this present world, and continue to live with confidence and joy—a patient spirit, sensing God's presence, and praying. But Paul goes beyond calling them to bring their needs to their Heavenly Father; he talks also about supplications and thanksgiving.

What are supplications? These are the cries of our hearts that we can hardly express with words. When we reach deeply into our soul, what do we find there? Sometimes we find far less than simple faith and trust in the Lord. Often, we find fears and anxiety. We might even see ugly responses to circumstances and to people when we are afraid. When we pour out to God the cries of our hearts, these are called supplications. This is all a part of a healthy relationship with God as we walk with Him through a fallen world.

GOD'S BIGGER ANSWER

When we bring to God whatever we find in the depth of our soul, all mixed with an attitude of thanksgiving, an amazing thing happens in our hearts.

> And the peace of God, which surpasses all understanding, will guard your hearts and your minds in Christ Jesus. (Philippians 4:7)

I would like to ask you to go back with me to the story of Daniel's three friends, Shadrach, Meshach and Abednego, before King Nebuchadnezzar of Babylon. They had refused to bow down to the image of gold he had made, and the king was threatening them with his burning fiery furnace. They had thought of two possible outcomes to this confrontation with the most powerful man in the most powerful kingdom in this world.

> If this be so, our God whom we serve is able to deliver us from the burning fiery furnace, and he will deliver us out of your hand, O king. But if not, be it known to you, O king, that we will not serve your gods or worship the golden image that you have set up. (Daniel 3:17–18)

They knew that God would either deliver them from Nebuchadnezzar's furnace, or He would deliver them to Himself through the furnace. God had a bigger answer in mind all the time. He would come into the furnace with them! When the king looked into the furnace, he saw four men, unbound, and "the fourth is like a son of the gods."

HIS PRESENCE IS BETTER THAN DELIVERANCE

The very Son of God, the pre-incarnate Christ, was in the furnace with Shadrach, Meshach and Abednego. God had done more than they asked Him to do, more than they hoped He would do. His presence with them in the flames was a bigger answer for them than deliverance from the furnace.

This is a very difficult thing for us as the children of God to learn. When we are in the flames of real life pain and pressure, we cry out to God for deliverance. In circumstances that threaten to overwhelm us, in relationships that bring more pain than we feel we can endure, we cry to our God for deliverance.

These are often places of terrible spiritual warfare in our minds. We cry out to God again and again, and still the circumstances and pain seem more than we can bear. Satan will remind us at these times that God always does less than we ask Him to do, always less than we hope He will do. But our God is always doing more than we can ever ask or imagine (Ephesians 3:20–21). He almost always has a bigger answer in mind than the cries of our hearts hope for. God's presence with us in the battle is a bigger answer than His deliverance from difficult circumstances. Sometimes in the dark days, it is difficult to remember that God is for us, and is always working toward our good.

Now, as we return to Paul's letter to the church at Philippi, we see him building on this wonderful truth we learn from Shadrach, Meshach and Abednego. His presence is not only a bigger answer than our deliverance, God's presence is a bigger answer than our understanding.

HIS PRESENCE IS BETTER THAN UNDERSTANDING

When we are in the furnace of great pain and confusion, experiencing more pressure than we feel we can endure, often our first cry to God is for deliverance. Then we are reminded that God is not primarily about changing circumstances; He desires to change the hearts of His people. He wants to use this situation to change us!

Where is the next place we tend to look for healing and hope? Well, if God would only explain to me why I am going through this trial, I could get through it! It is very difficult to learn that God's presence is a bigger answer than deliverance; it is even more challenging to learn that God's presence is a bigger answer than understanding.

When we place our hope in God and know that He is present with us, His peace guards our hearts. His peace goes far beyond our understanding! This place of settled confidence and rest is not dependent on knowing why; it is dependent on knowing God, and that He is here with us.

Some of us live with the illusion that when we get to heaven, we will have a personal conversation with God about all of the things in our lives that did not make sense to us at the times we experienced great loss, confusion and pain. He will then explain to us what was behind all of those things from His perspective. We will understand, and that understanding will become part of His healing of our lives.

That, of course will never happen. In fact, the moment we see the face of our beloved Lord, we will not be the least interested in any of those temporal questions. He will wipe away every tear, and our lives will be healed. All we will want to do then is to worship Him!

> Finally, brothers, whatever is true, whatever is honorable, whatever is just, whatever is pure, whatever is lovely, whatever is commendable, if there is any excellence, if there is anything worthy of praise, think about these things. What you have learned and received and heard and seen in me—practice these things, and the God of peace will be with you. (Philippians 4:8–9)

How does God set us free to give ourselves to the gospel in a real world, with real life experiences and relationships? He calls us to stand firm with one another, to know the joy that comes from inside out, to sense His presence which changes everything, and to bring the needs and cries of our hearts to Him.

What is the result of this process? His peace that surpasses understanding guards our hearts, and the God of peace will be with us. From that place of peace and confidence, the gospel flows to a needy world and brings hope to hurting people!

STUDY GUIDE

1. What qualifications does Paul give for being an example to follow? Support your answer from the text. Are you there yet? What needs to change before you can do that? Are your concerns valid or are they the accusations of the enemy? From the text, how do we know the difference?

2. Who are some of the models you have followed as you have sought to grow in maturity and ministry? Were they perfect? What about them qualified them to be a model for you? What are some of the things you have learned from them? Did they ever fail and not repent? From the text, how should we interact with a brother or sister at that point?

3. What about this world is so captivating? Do you find yourself longing for the "blessed hope" of the gospel in the return of Christ, the resurrection, and the presence of the Lord? What needs to happen in our hearts for our priorities to get and stay in perspective? Support your answer from the text.

4. As Paul begins chapter four, for the second time in the letter he calls his brothers and sisters to "stand firm." He is a prisoner in Rome and we are in a culture that is often uncomfortable for followers of Jesus. What does Paul encourage us to do in order to stand firm in the face of threats and intimidation?

5. Paul relentlessly calls his brothers and sisters to joy in this wonderful letter. But he is awaiting Nero's sword and they are living in very difficult financial circumstances. In what is he rejoicing? How is he asking them to join him in maintaining and perpetuating joy in others? Support your answer from the text. How have you experienced the joy of the Lord in difficult times in your life?

6. Using the text of Philippians define humility, standing firm and agreeing with one another. How would they each help Euodia and Syntyche resolve their differences? Why is it important for them to resolve their differences this way instead of just dealing with it, avoiding each other or parting ways? Have you ever seen this way of resolving differences in your church experience?

7. Find the places in Philippians where Paul describes that God's presence is a bigger answer than deliverance. What

struggle does this bring to the forefront for you? How does this encourage you? Take a moment to pray with each other in groups of two or three. Quote also the "Fiery Furnace" event in Daniel.

8. Find the places in Philippians where Paul describes God's presence as a bigger answer than an explanation we can understand? What reassurance does Paul give us that God's presence is bountiful enough to satisfy our needs and heal our hurts?

9. For Bill, looking for deliverance and explanations concerning life situations is linked with his love for this world. How do we move to seeking God's presence above the more temporal answers? How is maturing in this way important to the community of church and sharing the gospel?

10. Think of an experience or a time in your life when God's presence changed everything. Share that with your brothers and sisters, or just take some time in personal worship before the Lord for His bigger answer in your life!

PRAYER

Tell God that you know you are prone to seek deliverance and explanations even more than you seek His presence. Thank Him that His very presence enables you to stand firm in this world when everything shifts and changes around you. Pray that God will move your heart to hope more and more in Christ's return and the resurrection, and to look forward to the day you see His face, He wipes every tear away, and removes every hindrance this world has so you are fully free to worship Him forever and ever!

Not that I am speaking of being in need, for I have learned in whatever situation I am to be content. I know how to be brought low, and I know how to abound. In any and every circumstance, I have learned the secret of facing plenty and hunger, abundance and need.

Philippians 4:11–12

9

The Settled Confidence of Contentment

The Apostle Paul is a powerful model for the church at Philippi, and for you and me. He is facing many questions concerning his own future. Nero's imperial guards surround him, and the sword of the emperor threatens him daily. Paul knew well how deeply Nero hated Christians and saw them as a great threat to his kingdom. In spite of these circumstances, Paul knew the presence of His Lord and the peace His presence brings.

The churches of Macedonia, where the brothers and sisters of Philippi lived, were facing their own economic challenges. They struggled with poverty, and yet they helped make Paul's ministry possible as they supported him out of their meager resources. In spite of his own pressures and persecutions, Paul continued to give himself fully and freely to the gospel, and he calls the church at Philippi to follow his example.

This letter was not written to us, but it was surely written for us! Paul is teaching us as well how to give ourselves fully and freely to the gospel when we confront threats and difficult circumstances, or when we face fears and economic pressures. God's presence must produce our peace, as it did for Paul and his brothers and sisters in Macedonia, if we would be free to serve the Lord in the midst of this present darkness.

CONCERN AND OPPORTUNITY

Now, as Paul prepares to teach this church one of the most precious lessons of this letter, he thanks them once again for how they have helped to care for him:

> I rejoiced in the Lord greatly that now at length you have revived your concern for me. You were indeed concerned for me, but you had no opportunity. (Philippians 4:10)

Paul seems to be saying: "Where were you when I really needed you? At last you are concerned about me again!" But Paul knew in his heart that his beloved brothers and sisters had not waned in their love for him. They had been concerned all of this time, but they lacked an opportunity to help him.

Surely, the church at Philippi had continued to pray for the Apostle Paul. Epaphroditus had gone back and forth between Philippi and Rome, keeping the Philippians informed about Paul's conditions and his needs. What did it mean to "lack opportunity"? It may be that there was no way to get help to Paul at this time or to specifically meet his unique needs.

This reality is valuable for us to understand as well. As we give ourselves to the gospel, we need both concern and opportunity if we would be part of meeting the needs of the church around the world. It may be that God has laid a concern on our heart for a hurting church somewhere in the world, but, even as we pray for them, we do not know how to get them the help they need.

This text is a reminder for us to keep our eyes open to opportunities for the gospel. When we see a need to bring justice to the oppressed or to provide food for the hungry in the name of Jesus, this is part of proclaiming His name and His Kingdom. When we speak a word of encouragement to the sick and remind them of our Father's love even now, or when we bring the hope of forgiveness through the cross to those in despair, we are proclaiming the gospel.

As we learn more and more to do "Kingdom Praying," as Jesus encouraged His disciples to do in what we now call "The Lord's Prayer," praying that His Kingdom would come and His will be done on earth as it is in heaven, we need to pray more and more about praying! Part of "Kingdom Praying" is asking God to lay peoples and places in the world on our hearts, giving us concern for their needs, and then showing us how to walk with Him in the meeting of those needs. What opportunities might our God open to us as we seek to be of help to them in the gospel?

THAT GREAT CALENDAR VERSE!

> Not that I am speaking of being in need, for I have learned in whatever situation I am to be content. I know how to be brought low, and I know how to abound. In any and every circumstance, I have learned the secret of facing plenty and hunger, abundance and need. (Philippians 4:11–12)

Even as Paul thanks them for their concern and their gifts, he tells them how he has endured through the times of great need—even want. God enables him to be content with both plenty and hunger! He can handle times of abundance and times of need, because God is there with him, and Christ empowers him to endure and to flourish for the gospel.

> I can do all things through him who strengthens me. (Philippians 4:13)

We love to take wonderful Bible verses that bring great encouragement to our hearts and print them along with beautiful pictures on a monthly calendar. Every day we look at the picture and the verse, we sense once again the awe, the rest and the encouragement they bring. This is one of those verses.

Often, we take those verses out of context as we print them on our monthly calendars. Of course, this verse is true in every situation of life! When we face challenges and difficulties, we know that our God will provide for us all the strength we need through the resources of His Son.

But we must remember that if we take this verse out of its context and use it to preach a message other than the one Paul is preaching here, we are not being faithful to the text. We are then using the text to preach our message, rather than teaching the message of the author.

CONFIDENCE, PEACE AND REST

The message Paul is preaching to the church at Philippi is contentment. Because God gives Paul every resource of His Son in every life situation, Paul can handle times of need and times of abundance. He has learned to be content in either circumstance.

Contentment is one of God's most wonderful gifts to His children. Built on the promise of His presence which changes everything, and the peace that flows from the reality that He is here with us in every life situation, our God also promises to provide everything we need. This is a place where our hearts can rest!

Once again, we are confronted with the relationship between God's sovereignty and our rest. Because our God is all-powerful and rules over even the smallest detail of our lives, we can trust Him in everything. Contentment is living in that settled confidence in God, and in His care for us. He will be there when we are afraid. He will provide when we are in need. His steadfast love will carry us to places of security, abundance and rest.

God is setting us free from the taker/consumer mentality of this present age in order to give ourselves to His gospel. What is the alternative to contentment? We live always striving for more! We cannot be content because we are driven by our cravings for more success, more money, more sexual satisfaction, or more security.

A major part of this battle for many of God's children comes because of how many have misrepresented the gospel, as we discussed earlier. Rather than the biblical view of suffering now but glory later, false teachers have convinced us that we deserve glory now. Surely, because I am a child of God and He loves me, God would not want me to remain unhappy in this marriage, He would not want me to remain in this difficult life situation, He would not want me to remain in this battle with my health or my finances.

This can even become a deep spiritual battle in our relationship with God. Because our life expectations have become shaped by our culture and the voices of our enemy rather than the Bible, we can develop a demanding spirit before the Lord. We have given up everything to follow Him; there should be more for us in this Christian life than we have received!

FOUR TOOLS OF THE ENEMY

In his letter to the church at Philippi, Paul is actually setting before us four tools that Satan uses to steal away from us the freedom to orient everything we are and everything we have around the gospel of Christ.

- The first is relationships. Some of us are so resistant to God's process of building into us the heart of His Son that we are slow to become like Him. Even though God reveals the humility of His heart from the beginning of the scriptures to the end, our pride continues to control us. It is clear that He values mercy over justice, but we value justice over mercy. We will walk out of any relationship or split any church to preserve our "rightness." God lays down His life in order to pursue reconciliation, but we will hold onto our lives because justice is more important to us than relationships.

- Secondly, many of us have never been transformed by the "surpassing worthiness of Jesus." In fact, we have never been confronted with anything more valuable to us than those things at the center of our hearts right now. Our career, our marriage, our family, our sports, our hobbies, our money are worthy of our lives. Until we see the immeasurable beauty and value of the Son of God, nothing in our priorities will change.

- Thirdly, many of us are sincerely trying to serve the Lord while still dragging our past behind us. Every one of us has terrible places of sin and brokenness in our past. Like Paul, we need to forget what lies behind as we believe what God says about His cross and about our sin, and press on to become the man or woman God has called us to be, and to give ourselves to the gospel.

- The fourth is contentment. God wants to give to you and me the gift He gave to the apostle Paul. He provides this

149

place of settled confidence in His presence and in the gifts of His hand. God is asking us now: "Am I not enough for you? Are not the gifts I give sufficient for you? Do you still demand more?" We can never be free to orient all of life around the cross unless we are first content in our God and the provisions of His grace.

SHARING IN ONE ANOTHER'S TROUBLES

The gifts, prayers, love and encouragement that Paul received from the church at Philippi while he was in that Roman prison were a reminder of his Father's love for him. The grace that we bring to one another is a reflection of God's grace to us. Kindness is a uniquely Christian trait.

> Yet it was kind of you to share my trouble. And you Philippians yourselves know that in the beginning of the gospel, when I left Macedonia, no church entered into partnership with me in giving and receiving, except you only. (Philippians 4:14–15)

It is amazing that as broad as the ministry of the Apostle Paul was, the church at Philippi was the only church supporting him in those days. We read about his missionary journeys in the book of Acts, and we see Paul giving himself to church after church. There was surely something very special in Paul's relationship with the church at Philippi!

> Even in Thessalonica you sent me help for my needs once and again. Not that I seek the gift, but I seek the fruit that increases to your credit. (Philippians 4:16–17)

It is clear, too, that the financial support the Philippians provided for Paul was long term, ongoing and consistent. The purity of Paul's heart concerning finances is obvious as well when he talks of their account being "credited." If we heard these words from a television evangelist, our eyebrows might rise immediately, but we know that Paul's motives are pure.

His words are one more reminder that even though in this world we often say, concerning our resources in this world: "You can't take it with you." But what Paul is teaching us here is wonderful. There is an account in eternity with our name on it. We can't take it with us, but we can ship it on ahead!

> I have received full payment, and more. I am well supplied, having received from Epaphroditus the gifts you sent, a fragrant offering, a sacrifice acceptable and pleasing to God. (Philippians 4:18)

THE FOUNTAIN FROM WHICH CONTENTMENT FLOWS

Part of the way we invest in eternity is to ask God to lay the concerns for hurting people, and the needs of the church around the world, on our heart. Then we pray that He would provide an opportunity for us to help meet their needs. Our freedom to participate with them flows from the contentment we find in God and the gifts from His hand, and His promise to meet every need we have.

> And my God will supply every need of yours according to his riches in glory in Christ Jesus. To our God and Father be glory forever and ever. Amen. (Philippians 4:19–20)

As the Apostle Paul thanks the church at Philippi for being a part of God meeting his needs, he assures them that God will supply all of their needs as well. Our Father's ability to care for His children is limitless because His resources are beyond measure. He meets every need of our lives out of His glorious riches in His Son!

When we read these words from the Apostle Paul, we are reminded of the encouragement of the Lord Jesus. Near the beginning of His ministry, Christ was calling His disciples to seek Him and His Kingdom with all of their hearts. How can we live fully focused on the Kingdom when we live in a physical world with real physical needs?

> Therefore I tell you, do not be anxious about your life, what you will eat or what you will drink, nor about your body, what you will put on. Is not life more than food, and the body more than clothing? (Matthew 6:25)

Life is more than food, and the body more than clothing. Jesus used the birds as an illustration for us. They, too, live with physical needs, and yet God cares for them. His children are even more valuable to Him than birds, and He will care for them as well.

> Look at the birds of the air: they neither sow nor reap nor gather into barns, and yet your heavenly Father feeds them. Are you not of more value than they? And which of you by being anxious can add a single hour to his span of life? (Matthew 6:26–27)

God's creatures live without anxiety because He cares for them. How much can we change our lives by being anxious about the cares of this world? We cannot even add one hour to the span of our life!

> And why are you anxious about clothing? Consider the lilies of the field, how they grow: they neither toil nor spin, yet I tell you, even Solomon in all his glory was not arrayed like one of these. (Matthew 6:28–29)

The Lord Jesus then talked about the freedom of flowers. They are not consumed with producing in this world, but God cares for them, and their beauty is unsurpassed.

> But if God so clothes the grass of the field, which today is alive and tomorrow is thrown into the oven, will he not much more clothe you, O you of little faith? Therefore do not be anxious, saying, "What shall we eat?" or "What shall we drink?" or "What shall we wear?" (Matthew 6:30–31)

In light of God's care for flowers and birds, why should we be concerned about whether He will meet the needs of our lives? Why should we be consumed with these daily pressures when our Father loves us far more than He loves creatures and plants?

> For the Gentiles seek after all these things, and your heavenly Father knows that you need them all. (Matthew 6:32)

After all these things the nations run, Jesus said, but your Father knows what you need. This reality sets us free from running after what we need each day, and enables us to focus on what is eternal.

> But seek first the kingdom of God and his righteousness, and all these things will be added to you. (Matthew 6:33)

This is the fountain from which contentment flows. We can live with a settled confidence in our Father's care because He has promised to meet every need of our lives. Out of His glorious riches in Christ Jesus, God will provide for us. That place of contentment sets us free to give our lives away and to orient every resource around the cross.

THE END OF THE GOSPEL

As we come to the close of our walk through Paul's letter to the church at Philippi, we are reminded of his focus on the gospel in his encouragement to his beloved brothers and sisters. Every relationship, every resource, attitude and passion of Paul's life was focused on the gospel of Christ, and he is teaching this church how to live in that same way. The ministry of reconciliation was at the very center of Paul's heart.

It is important for us to remember, however, that the salvation of souls is not the end of the gospel. We so desire our loved ones to be saved; the thought of friends and neighbors going into eternity without God's forgiveness through the blood of His Son brings great pain to our hearts. There is a higher purpose, however, as we orient every resource, attitude and passion around the cross. The goal of the gospel is the glory of God and worship of the Lamb!

Paul made this very clear as he closed his letter to his beloved brothers and sisters in Philippi:

> To our God and Father be glory forever and ever. Amen. (Philippians 4:20)

The Apostle John picked up Paul's theme as God revealed to him the fulfillment of time, eternity, and every purpose of our

Father's heart. He describes a scene around His eternal throne. In that picture, we see the living creatures in His presence, the elders, and the Lamb that had been slain. It hardly seems possible for the apostle to put into words that we can understand the heavenly scenes revealed by the Spirit of God.

> And they sang a new song, saying, "Worthy are you to take the scroll and to open its seals, for you were slain, and by your blood you ransomed people for God from every tribe and language and people and nation, and you have made them a kingdom and priests to our God, and they shall reign on the earth." (Revelation 5:9–10)

Along with the Apostle John we are captivated by the worship! As we hear the song that is sung by those around the throne of God, we are reminded of one of Paul's great themes in his letter to the church at Philippi: the worthiness of Jesus gives birth to the song in the throne room.

> Then I looked, and I heard around the throne and the living creatures and the elders the voice of many angels, numbering myriads of myriads and thousands of thousands, saying with a loud voice, "Worthy is the Lamb who was slain, to receive power and wealth and wisdom and might and honor and glory and blessing!" (Revelation 5:11–12)

It is very difficult for us to even try to visualize this scene— the living creatures in God's presence, the elders around His throne, myriads of angels, and those from every tribe, tongue, people and nation worshiping together the worthiness of God's glorious Son! Jesus is worthy not only because He was slain and purchased for His Father the inheritance of the nations, He is worthy because He is the eternal and only begotten Son, the Lord of Lords, and the center of our God's every affection and purpose.

> And I heard every creature in heaven and on earth and under the earth and in the sea, and all that is in them, saying, "To him who sits on the throne and to the Lamb be blessing and honor and glory and might forever and ever!"

And the four living creatures said, "Amen!" and the elders fell down and worshiped. (Revelation 5:13–14)

SING IT NOW!

We will be there in the throne room on the day this song is sung. We will join with the angels, God's creatures and His elders, and with the nations as we together lift high our God, the Lord Jesus Christ. We will be forever caught up in exalting the beauty, power, wisdom wealth and honor of the risen Christ.

This will become our forever, favorite song. We will never tire of singing this song! Over and over throughout the realms of eternity, we will want the echoes of this song to be heard by not only those in the throne room, but anywhere in God's universe, by anyone who has ears to hear. Our passions that were ignited when we saw the surpassing worthiness of Jesus will only be satisfied as we sing this song to Him, to one another, and to every creature as we call them to join us in worshiping Him.

In Paul's letter to the church at Philippi, he is challenging them, and us, to sing now the song that we will sing forever. Rather than waiting until we get to heaven, the apostle is calling us to make this the song of our lives right now: Worthy is the Lamb!

Sing it now! Sing this song with your money. Sing it in your marriage. Sing it in the attitudes of your heart. Sing it in your relationships with one another. Sing it every day, in every way, so that the world that is watching might join us in worship. Worthy is the Lamb who was slain!

STUDY GUIDE

1. When and why does Paul say the Philippian church gave to him? Are these patterns you see in your own giving? What will help you grow in your generosity? Support your answer from the text.

2. In order to be effective givers, we need both concern and opportunity. How do humility, standing firm and unity play a role in giving? How have you sought the Lord in these areas of your own ministry giving?

3. What are the elements of your prayer life? Using the text list the elements of Paul's prayer life. What are the discrepancies between your prayer life and the one Paul describes? In groups of two or three name two things that you need to change about your prayer life. Set reminders on your calendars to encourage each other throughout the week to grow in these areas.

4. How does the cultural understanding of Philippians 4:13 and Paul's explanation of it differ? Why is this distinction important? How does this change the way we stand firm, are humble and remain unified?

5. Explain Paul's definition of contentment from the text. Where in your life do you struggle with living in this way?

6. Expectations for life—yours and God's. How often are these two sets of expectations congruent? How often are they at odds? According to Philippians how do you know when they are congruent or at odds? What can we do to grow in making our expectations congruent with God's expectations for our lives, the lives of our loved ones and the life of His church?

7. Define from the text of Philippians the four tools of the enemy through which he would steal away our freedom to give ourselves to Christ. In which of these do you battle most as you seek to give yourself to advance Christ?

8. Compare Paul's teaching on contentment to Jesus teaching how God cares for us (Matthew 6). What areas of your life are easy to trust to Jesus's care? What areas are difficult to trust to Jesus's care? How can you grow in your trust and therefore contentment in Jesus?

9. According to Philippians, what is the point of the gospel? How is this important in the way we choose to trust God now?

10. The eternal song: "Worthy is the Lamb." Take some time to describe how Paul was "singing" this song from his jail cell, sharing how others in ministry with him were "singing" it with their example and calling the Philippians to "sing" it as well. How are you "singing" that song in the present circumstances of your marriage, finances, career, children, neighborhood, friendships, etc.? How can you sing it more?

PRAYER

Thank your God that He has committed Himself to your care and promised to give to you everything you need. Ask Him to give you more and more that spirit of contentment in Him and in the gifts from His hand so that you can give yourself to Him, rather than living in fear or in the pressure to strive for more stuff or security. Pray that God would stir in you a deeper passion for the worthiness of Jesus so that you can sing now the song you will sing forever with God's angels, and with those from every tribe, tongue, people and nation!

Scripture Index

Leadership Resources
International

If you have been encouraged by this book, you m consider using it in a small group or class in your chu You might also consider inviting Bill to your next chu missions conference, or any weekend you want to focus on gospel, to speak on the themes of this book.

Our desire is to magnify God in the eyes of His people that they may stand in awe, wonder and worship before I and be transformed in His presence. We do this as we bring encouragement of the scriptures to churches, pastors missions. The largest aspect of our work is encouraging equipping pastors in the developing world who often have l formal training for the ministry. These ministries take p throughout Latin America, Africa, Asia, the South Pac Europe and the former Soviet Union. We invite your church partner with us in one of these training times.

For more information about our conferences or materi contact:

Leadership Resources
12575 South Ridgeland Avenue
Palos Heights, IL 60463
(800) 980–2226
www.leadershipresources.org

25 Praying about Praying
49-50 Because He is worth it
58-60 Transformed Hearts; Transformed Relationships

71-75
96-98 The Balanced Christian Life

Made in the USA
Columbia, SC
12 January 2020

86571926R00091